"When it comes to small groups, Steve is not just a theoretical expert, he is a consummate practitioner. Groups have the power to change lives; this book has the power to change groups."

John Ortberg, senior pastor, Menlo Park Presbyterian Church; author, *The Me I Want to Be*

"*Leading Small Groups with Purpose* is the one book on small groups that you simply must get into the hands of every one of your small group leaders. Biblical, intentional, and focused, this book is full of real-world advice on the practical matters of running a group. After almost thirty years in ministry, Steve Gladen gives your leaders the information they need not only to guide their groups but also to develop their members toward maturity and health. Want a healthier church? Develop healthier small groups. Start here."

Rick Warren, Saddleback Church

"I wish this book was in the hands of every small group leader in America. The power of God's work in community is not in the form (small groups); it is in the function (the purposes) lived out in deep, authentic relationships. Steve Gladen's biblical focus, practical instruction, and game-day experience make this an essential for all of us committed to transformation, not simply transmission of information."

Chip Ingram, senior pastor, Venture Christian Church; president, Living on the Edge

"Healthy small group communities are a key component of today's thriving churches. And healthy leadership is the key to healthy groups. In these pages Steve lays out a step-by-step plan for keeping both groups and their leaders healthy and vibrant. *Leading Small Groups with Purpose* is a must-read!"

Nelson Searcy, lead pastor, The Journey Church; founder, Church Leader Insights; author, *Engage*

"I'm so glad Steve Gladen wrote this book! *Leading Small Groups with Purpose* gives us an incredible resource that should be in the hands of every small group leader. It's filled with practical insights and time-tested wisdom on how to lead a group to be effective and balanced. His comprehensive approach gives clear direction on how to achieve health and mission in community. Don't miss it!"

Jud Wilhite, senior pastor, Central Christian Church, Las Vegas; author, *Torn*

"More than a how-to manual, *Leading Small Groups with Purpose* captures the heart of its author, Steve Gladen, and the thriving small group ministry at Saddleback Church. Steve's heart has always been for the local church to experience authentic community through healthy small groups. His honest, transparent, and helpful leadership offers life lessons in this book that will encourage you whether you are just starting out on your small group journey, desiring to increase the health of an existing small group, or searching for tools to develop future leaders. You won't be disappointed!"

Kerry Shook, senior pastor, Woodlands Church

"I have personally watched Steve Gladen tirelessly and meticulously work out small group architecting for the local church. His experience and integrity with the process is unmatched. The body of Christ owes him a BIG thank-you for shortening the process for all who read this book, learning the painful lessons for us, and passing on to us a blueprint for small group community that produces church health."

Kenny Luck, president and founder, Every Man
Ministries; pastor of men, Saddleback Church

"*Leading Small Groups with Purpose* will inspire and inform you with fresh ideas and practical information that flow from Steve Gladen's wealth of expertise. If you want to see your small group grow, this book is for you. Thanks, Steve—for this book, for your huge heart, and especially for all your help!"

Steve Mawston, Connect Groups pastor, Hillsong Church Australia

"Healthy people in healthy small groups is a sign of a very healthy church. Fewer people on the planet know more about building healthy small groups than Steve Gladen. *Leading Small Groups with Purpose* is about intentional small group leadership. Steve brings leaders into a fresh commitment to personal ownership for internal growth, passionate responsibility for outward mission, and intentional apprenticing for reproducing leaders.

Scott Hodge, pastor, The Orchard Community, Aurora, Illinois

"Some authors write about small group theory. Steve Gladen writes from the trenches of small group life and leadership. He has lived every word. If you've dreamed of moving from a safe, sanitized group of navel gazers to a strategic group of purposeful disciples, this book is for you."

Gene Appel, senior pastor, Eastside Christian
Church, Fullerton, California

"God has built something truly remarkable in Southern California. And he has used Steve Gladen and Rick Warren to do it. For the first time in print, Steve lays out what every small group leader needs to know in order to lead a healthy group. This is a truly helpful addition to the small group leader's arsenal!"

Bill Search, author, *Simple Small Groups*

LEADING
Small Groups
with
PURPOSE

LEADING
Small Groups
with
PURPOSE

Everything
You Need to Lead
a Healthy Group

Steve Gladen

BakerBooks

a division of Baker Publishing Group
Grand Rapids, Michigan

Published by Baker Books
a division of Baker Publishing Group
P.O. Box 6287, Grand Rapids, MI 49516-6287
www.bakerbooks.com

Printed in the United States of America

Library of Congress Cataloging-in-Publication Data
Gladen, Steve, 1960–
    Leading small groups with purpose : everything you need to lead a healthy group / Steve Gladen.
        p.   cm.
    Includes index.
    ISBN 978-0-8010-1380-5 (cloth)
    1. Church group work. 2. Small groups—Religious aspects—Christianity.
I. Title.
BV652.2.G484 2012
259—dc23   2011030791

Unless otherwise indicated, Scripture quotations are from the Holy Bible, New International Version®. NIV®. Copyright © 1973, 1978, 1984 by Biblica, Inc.™ Used by permission of Zondervan. All rights reserved worldwide. www.zondervan.com

Scripture quotations labeled Message are from *The Message* by Eugene H. Peterson, copyright © 1993, 1994, 1995, 2000, 2001, 2002. Used by permission of NavPress Publishing Group. All rights reserved.

Scripture quotations labeled NASB are from the New American Standard Bible®, copyright © 1960, 1962, 1963, 1968, 1971, 1972, 1973, 1975, 1977, 1995 by The Lockman Foundation. Used by permission.

Scripture quotations labeled NCV are from the New Century Version®. Copyright © 1987, 1988, 1991 by Word Publishing, a division of Thomas Nelson, Inc. Used by permission. All rights reserved.

Scripture quotations labeled NLT are from the *Holy Bible*, New Living Translation, copyright © 1996, 2004, 2007 by Tyndale House Foundation. Used by permission of Tyndale House Publishers, Inc., Carol Stream, Illinois 60188. All rights reserved.

Scripture quotations labeled TNIV are from the Holy Bible, Today's New International Version®. TNIV®. Copyright © 2001, 2005 by Biblica, Inc.™ Used by permission of Zondervan. All rights reserved worldwide. www.zondervan.com

The internet addresses, email addresses, and phone numbers in this book are accurate at the time of publication. They are provided as a resource. Baker Publishing Group does not endorse them or vouch for their content or permanence.

12   13   14   15   16   17   18   7   6   5   4   3   2   1

To each of you who lead community, not for the glory, fame, or status, but to play a role in God's kingdom purpose to see people live out the Great Commission and Great Commandment.

Contents

Foreword

When Jesus wanted to change the world, he did not start with a political movement, a media campaign, a powerful army, or a global network. He started with a small group.

Take your small group from a gathering of nice folks who meet to pray, study the Bible, and support one another—all worthwhile and wonderful pursuits—to a body of believers with the power to be agents of the kingdom of God.

Steve Gladen pours his twenty-plus years of shepherding and shaping small groups into this one-of-a-kind toolbox, designed to equip you and your group for the kind of dynamic growth that can turn ordinary people into water-walking disciples of the living and breathing Word of God.

Nothing has the power to change us like authentic experiences with God, and I've seen this kind of transformation happen time and again as people do life together in small group communities. In this book, you'll learn how to build the kinds of small groups that challenge one another to become Christ in this world, reaching out with his hands and arms to help those who are suffering, willing to walk with his feet wherever he might call you in order to bring his gospel of hope to the lost.

As pastor of more than 3,500 Saddleback Church small groups, Steve has mastered the principles he presents in these pages. You'll discover through his trademark honesty and see-through, guy-next-door humor that even pastors have spiritual disasters, and that often if it weren't for our spouses, we might all have had to turn in our Christian cards long ago. It's what we learn along the way and how we apply God's lessons that matter.

Here are a few of the jewels you'll find in this book that will make you agree it deserves a permanent place in your library:

1. God is intentional, and you have a purpose.
    See yourself through God's eyes.
    Understand the power of mentorship and community.
    Leadership involves knowing who you are in Christ, prioritizing people, and acknowledging that God trusts you with his most valuable treasure—each other!
2. God has a purpose for your group, and discovering what it is begins with you.
    God's purposes for his church are his purposes for your group.
    We need to define success and achieve balance in our groups.
    Learn helpful, reliable, time-tested small group guidelines.
3. Where do we begin?
    Take a Spiritual Health Assessment—like a regular physical.
    Develop a Spiritual Health Plan that acknowledges weak areas and plans for growth.
    Gain insight into effective leadership—how to develop an intentional pathway for development.
4. Where two or more are gathered . . .
    Understand the barriers to join—know what they are and how to tear them down.

Learn common questions and some answers to prepare you for them.

Discover where to start and how to see times of
struggle as opportunities for growth.

5. Fellowship: build a healthy foundation.

Create an environment that encourages going deeper.

Understand the "after group" meeting, when connections are often built.

Keep the agenda from driving out the Holy Spirit.

6. Discipleship: encourage and develop spiritual growth.

What or who has made a difference in your growth?

How could you impact others in that way?

The goal of discipleship is transformation—it's not
about getting through the lesson each week.

Keep the paralysis of fear from trapping you "in
the boat."

7. Ministry: mobilize your group members toward serving
opportunities that are right for them and achieve your
group's purpose.

Help members find their serving sweet spot.

Encourage shared ownership.

Don't lead alone.

Make ministry a regular part of your group experience.

8. Evangelism: reach outside your group.

Availability is the key to evangelism.

Manage group growth.

Cast visions, reach out, and pray to the Lord of the
harvest.

9. Worship: experience God together.

Give expressive and reflective suggestions.

Share God stories.

Be willing to pray in the moment.

Understand the heart of worship.

Experience God moments.

10. Keep your group on track—recognize obstacles and opportunities.
    Learn how to navigate a lesson.
    Learn conflict resolution—a biggie!
    Care for the Extra Grace Required people.

Henry Cloud said once that people are God's Plan A for changing people. And there is no Plan B. Nothing shapes our lives like the women and men closest to us. I am so glad Steve wrote a handbook for people-shaping. So enough with the prelims—it's time to get to work!

John Ortberg
Senior Pastor, Menlo Park Presbyterian Church

Acknowledgments

Many thanks to:

The *many* pastors, small group leaders, and members who played a huge role in my life even before small group ministry as a career ever entered my mind. Thanks for your role in shaping me for kingdom service.

Rick and Kay Warren, who have poured their wisdom into me since 1983 without even knowing it. Your constant dedication to ministry, pastoral families, and the health of the church are overwhelming. You are the same on the platform as you are in person. Your sacrifice makes this book possible and the small group ministry of Saddleback Church what it is. I wish everyone could get a glimpse of the pastor I know day in and day out. You are my pastor. Thanks for leading!

Cheryl Shireman, who wrote an email with a helpful critique of our program that led her to become part of the solution and the right arm of the Small Group Network. Her passion for writing and making sense of senseless thoughts has been the salvation for me and this book. She read my mind and brought this book to life! Cheryl, you are a godsend.

Jeanine Feld, who has lived this journey more than most by working next to me since December 1998, making my ministry more effective for God's kingdom. Your unseen hours devoted to Saddleback Church, the Small Group Conferences, and the Small Group Network are the untold story. Your reward is truly in heaven.

Brett Eastman, who brought me to Saddleback. What started out as a lunch turned into the ride of a lifetime! Thanks for believing in me.

The small group team in Lake Forest that manages this campus and the central support to our other campuses: Shelly Antol, Tom Atkins, Jim Brewington, Jean Bushong, Jennifer Cantwell, John Caputo, Tom Crick, Dee Eastman, Debbie Eaton, Jeanine Feld, John Gaudette, Karen Fera, Kari Hollerbach, Kerri Johnson, Wayne Jones, Deanna Kaech, Lisa Law, Kenny Luck, Rommel Manio, Efraim Meulenberg, Helen Mitchell, Solange Montoya, Todd Olthoff, Tina Pretsch, Chris Reed, Laura Sullivan, Maggie Voelker, Ron Wilbur, and Rick Zeiger. And the regional campuses' small group teams: Rick Bradford, Randy Craft, Jeremiah Goley, Derek Robinson, Cynthia Ross, Jeffrey Slipp, James Valencia, and David Williamson. To the BDTITLE: thanks for the mentoring, ministry, moments, and fun as we figure this out.

The Small Group Network Domestic and International leadership: Ed Applegate, Alastair Bate, Danny Bennett, Vinnie Cappetta, Jay Daniell, Matt Hodgson, David Hull, Mark Kendall, Mark Mehlig, Michael Moore, Eddie Mosley, Cheryl Shireman, Jon Weiner, Joe Windham, and Ron Youtsey, who cover the network with me, and to the area and local leadership, who make the network strong so that nobody stands alone.

Those who read the manuscript and gave suggestions that made this book better: Christi Hamilton, Carolyn Taketa, Rex Minor, Rick Howerton, Rick Zeiger, Greig Gladen, and Nita Bukowski.

Kenny Luck, Katie Brazelton, and Caleb Anderson for their contributions to chapter 1. Thanks for helping me develop the framework of the four questions of leadership.

The more than 3,500 small group leaders of Saddleback Church who week in and week out shape the destinations of thousands of folks one life at a time.

My small group, who have lived this crazy journey with Lisa and me: Bill and Elaine Crane, John and Janet Hertogh, Gina and Tyra Rikimaru. Our families are forever knit together.

My parents, who took a risk in their fifties to follow Christ and who are waiting for us in heaven—party on! To my brothers Kurt, Greig, Todd, Mark, and my brave sister, Nita; I love life with you and wish geography wasn't between us. Move to Southern California!

Lisa, Erika, and Ethan, whom I would die for and who are the reason I get up in the morning. Lisa, you cheer me on and give me grace. Since 1988 you have believed in me and this book. You sacrifice more than anyone knows; you are the strength behind our marriage, family, and ministry. I love you! Erika and Ethan, you bring a smile and a glimpse into the future. I pray for your growth in the Lord and impact for his kingdom. Live strong for him!

To Jesus Christ, who strengthens me and makes this whole work possible.

About Your Complimentary Code

This book includes a little bonus. When you purchased the book, you also received a complimentary code allowing you to try out a small group tool that I think you'll enjoy. In fact, I believe it is a fantastic tool for fostering healthy groups, and we've had great success with it at Saddleback. It's called Small Group Insights. This innovative, online tool is quick, easy, and effective.

Simply go to www.smallgroupinsights.com and use the complimentary code that you'll find on the reverse side of the dust jacket of this book. You'll then answer a series of questions that will take you less than ten minutes. Instantly you'll receive a personal report detailing your unique group style. You'll find that you are primarily a Talker, a Doer, a Thinker, or a Listener. But you'll discover far more than that. The report includes a three-step process you can use within your own group.

While the cost of this tool is minimal, I've arranged to supply your other group members with a discount for their codes. So if you choose to use Small Group Insights in your group, be sure to use this discount coupon: **SGN**. This discount will work whether you are purchasing additional blocks of codes for your members or your group members are purchasing individual codes for themselves. If you have trouble with your code, email information@smallgroupinsights.com.

Introduction

The Purpose of This Book

Be shepherds of God's flock that is under your care, serving as overseers—not because you must, but because you are willing, as God wants you to be; not greedy for money, but eager to serve; not lording it over those entrusted to you, but being examples to the flock. And when the Chief Shepherd appears, you will receive the crown of glory that will never fade away.

1 Peter 5:2–4

Good leaders make people feel that they're at the very heart of things, not at the periphery. Everyone feels that he or she makes a difference to the success of the organization. When that happens people feel centered, and that gives their work meaning.

Warren Bennis

Flash back with me to 1977. I was a junior in high school. I was also a new follower of Christ. What was high school like for me? Was I an ESPN 150 Top Pick? Not even close. Getting ready to attend my first prom? No again. I was actually a late bloomer in *many* ways. A scholar? Nope. I had to struggle just to get C's and B's. Luckily, gym class was always there to pull up my GPA! But surely, I was a sought-after young Christian leader, right? Not even close. I think the phrase that best describes me during that time is "in the background." I was not a part of the *in crowd*, the Who's Who, the pretty people, or those who were invited to parties. And worse yet, I had no plans for the future. I was clueless. My dad was in business, so I had a vague notion that I would head down that path too. That summed up my goals at the time. I enjoyed my life and basically just took it one day at a time.

Enter a man named Ron Swiger. Ron was an adult in my church who took me under his wing without my ever realizing he was doing it. Our church didn't have small groups, but they did have Sunday school and a bus ministry. (Google it—it was a phenomenon in the 1970s.) That Sunday school functioned much like a small group, and the bus ministry included serving and evangelism. Although the methodologies I use today are different, I realize now what a powerful role Ron played in my life.

He made sure I was involved and gave me a place to belong. He asked me to be an assistant in the bus ministry on his bus. He spent time with me. He did ministry in such a way that I wanted to be like him. He was also my Sunday school teacher. He was far ahead of his time and was a master at promoting growth in his students. He taught me to pray. He challenged me to give back to God. He taught the Bible in a relevant way. Most importantly, he modeled what he taught. That Sunday school class was probably the best-disguised small group of the day. We didn't just learn biblical facts; we learned how to live life together. We had parties, interacted with the greater church, did outreach events together, and learned to challenge each other to deal with the dark areas of our hearts. Were we perfect? No. Did I apply everything I learned to my life? No. But did that class, despite its weaknesses, make an impact in my life? Yes!

When Ron stepped out of the role as my mentor, another man stepped in—Bill Brown. God used him to build on the foundation Ron had started. During my years in high school, despite my clueless nature, Bill planted a seed for ministry. That seed would not bloom for almost eight years, but it was still firmly planted. And I owe a lot to those two men.

What's the moral of the story? If you have this book in your hands, chances are someone took a risk on you. Someone invited you to be in his or her small group or asked you to lead a small group. Whatever the case may be, someone believed in you. *You* may not have seen your potential, but that person did. And so does God. I hope this book will help you develop a healthy small group—a vital community of friends.

PART 1

Before You Begin Your Group

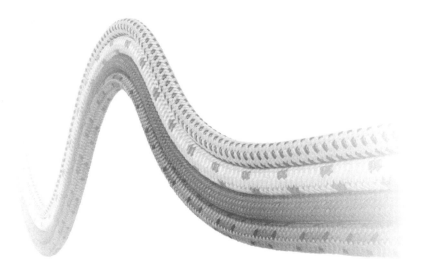

You Are Part of God's Plan

Discovering Your Purpose

I came to you in weakness and fear, and with much trembling. My message and my preaching were not with wise and persuasive words, but with a demonstration of the Spirit's power, so that your faith might not rest on men's wisdom, but on God's power.

1 Corinthians 2:3–5

Great minds have purposes, others have wishes.

Washington Irving

If you are reading this page, two things are probably true:

1. You are leading, or part of, a small group.
2. You are feeling not as qualified to lead or help a small group as you'd like.

27

And before you get mad at me, let me tell you a secret: I don't feel qualified to lead a small group either. But that's okay. We don't have to be qualified; we just have to have God on our side. If he has called you to lead a small group, then he will give you the ability to do so. The key is staying connected to him, continuing to seek his will, and then surrendering to it. God will always show you the way. "Trust in the LORD with all your heart and lean not on your own understanding; in all your ways acknowledge him, and he will make your paths straight" (Proverbs 3:5–6). Of course it is always your choice whether to follow him.

One more thing is probably true as well. You most likely fall into one of four categories:

1. You just started leading a small group and already regret saying you would. The church leader caught you at a weak moment. If you have not had your first meeting yet, the thought of it makes you slightly sick to your stomach. Before the first group starts, you wonder whether anyone will show up. Or you have already had a few meetings, and every week you feel slightly nauseous before everyone arrives.

2. You have been leading a small group for some time now, but you feel as though you are missing something. Your group meets regularly, but there seems to be a lack of focus and purpose. You aren't really sure what you thought a small group would be like, but this isn't it. Your group is in a rut, and you need to get out of that rut.

3. You have been leading a small group since the dawn of time, and you're bored to death. You like the members of your group, maybe you even love them, but your group meetings seem more like social gatherings than a meeting of empowered disciples. You are bored with the studies, and if truth be told, you'd rather just hang out and enjoy the party.

28

4. You can't imagine life without your group. You look forward to group meetings and even meet with group members outside of group time. Deep bonds have developed between members. You sense that God is doing something here, and you are ready to continue moving to that next level.

No matter where you are in your journey with your small group, I believe this book will help take you, your group, and the individual members of your group to the next level. If a group is centered on a purpose and led by a focused leader, there is no greater tool for spiritual growth than the small group. From the beginning, God has used small groups of men and women to change the world. That has not changed. Your small group, under intentional leadership and the direction of God, is a force to be reckoned with. The potential of a small group of God-focused people is simply astounding. Matter of fact, it carried the church for the first three hundred years of its existence!

God has used small groups of men and women to change the world. That has not changed.

If you have been leading a group for some time, as you read this book you're going to say, "Wow! That's a great idea." Or, "I wish I had done that earlier." The last thing I want you to do, however, is feel that you have been doing something wrong. On the other hand, some of you are at point A and just trying to learn how to get to point B. The key is to keep learning and sharing our ideas with each other so we can continue to take our group and our group members to the next level. Wherever you are, and wherever I am, we can learn from each other.

As you learn from this book, don't try to implement it all within the next month. Understand that developing a healthy group takes time. Just concentrate on one step at a time.

Trust God

When I was called into ministry, between my junior and senior years of high school, everything in me said I was not qualified. I have a bit of a learning disability. When I am thinking quickly, or speaking quickly, I tend to drop letters or switch numbers or words around, which made school a real challenge. I excelled in math and science, but I really struggled with English because I was always switching or dropping letters. Reading was a chore. I made it through high school, college, and graduate school, but every step of the way I felt as though God had the wrong person. Couldn't he see that I was clearly *not* qualified to be in ministry? Somewhere near the end of my graduate program, in a moment of frustration and fear, I came across 1 Corinthians 2:3–5:

> I came to you in weakness and fear, and with much trembling. My message and my preaching were not with wise and persuasive words, but with a demonstration of the Spirit's power, so that your faith might not rest on men's wisdom, but on God's power.

Of course, I had read it many times before, but on that day it seemed to have been written especially for me. I suddenly realized God did not need my eloquence. Wise and persuasive words were not at the top of God's list for success. He needed my obedience. He would give me the strength to overcome any shortcomings I might have. And he has and will continue to do so.

Share Your Weaknesses

One of the most important things I have learned about leadership is that people love you more for your faults and weaknesses than for your strengths. The world tells us a leader is strong, confident, and bold. But the Bible tells us that some of the greatest leaders of all time (Moses, David, Joseph) were weak, reluctant, and afraid. As a leader, the most significant thing you can share with the members of your group is your weakness. If you are afraid to pray out loud, tell them. If you don't know the answer to a question, don't try to bluff your way through it—admit that you don't know. Then look it up and come back with the answer the following week.

When I was home from college one summer, I was helping with the youth department of a local church. Mike and Carol were the leaders, and I was just there to do whatever. I learned later that their job was to give me confidence. They thought I could do no wrong; I thought all I could do was wrong. They knew I was called into ministry, but I was just halfway through my long run of excuses. They used that summer to help me do one thing: lead a group. Week after week they taught me to be myself. I didn't have to know it all. I didn't have to be one up on everyone. I did have to be secure in the Lord and trust him to use my testimony and giftedness. Each week they modeled transparency and authenticity. I watched and listened in amazement as their group grew and loved them more with every week, even though they didn't have it all together. They showed me that weakness can be strength. The people in your small group will not let down their guard and share their weaknesses until you are willing to do the same. Model the behavior you expect from them.

Develop Your Empathy Quotient

"If there is any great secret to success in life," industrialist Henry Ford said, "it lies in the ability to put yourself in the other person's place and to see things from his point of view." Ford could have been talking about leading a healthy small group. After all, if a leader doesn't develop the capacity to step inside the skin of each group member and see through their eyes, the group will surely suffer. Guaranteed. Why? Because empathy is essential to creating a safe place. Empathy opens a person's spirit. Empathy cultivates grace.

The challenge for a group leader, of course, is that empathy doesn't come easy. More often than not, we assume people think and feel the way we do. But they don't. God designed each of us with differences. Each person in your group is unique. But in time, with shared experiences and by asking good questions, the astute group leader begins to recognize and appreciate those differences. Indeed, these differences become the delight of the group.

That's why I'm a fan of the online tool called Small Group Insights. This simple tool allows a group leader (as well as group members) to uncover and better understand each member's hardwiring. Among other things, it's a tool for empathy. For example, if you are inclined to be a Talker and you have a Thinker in your group, your impulse may be to conclude that this person isn't engaged in the group like you are. But once you empathize—once you step into their shoes and understand their personal style—you may discover that they are plugged into the group process more than anyone else. They simply express it differently.

Studies have shown that most of us think we empathize better than we actually do. So do yourself a favor and check out www.smallgroupinsights.com. I think you'll be glad you did.

Four Questions of Leadership

The fundamental issue that determines the extent to which God can bless your leadership is your heart. If you and I are honest with ourselves and with God, it will not take us very long to identify areas of our hearts and lives that are divided, self-centered, and generally not honoring to God. If we leave our hearts unmanaged, they will eventually be our downfall.

Before you can be an effective spiritual leader, you must be surrendered as a follower of Christ. The act of surrendering to Christ is a lifelong process as his Spirit grows you toward maturity. As a leader, you will need to answer four basic questions along the way.

1. Identity: Who Am I?

When Moses was an infant, Pharaoh decreed that every firstborn child of the Israelites be killed. Moses's mother disobeyed and put tiny baby Moses in a basket, sending him afloat in the Nile River. Ironically, Pharaoh's daughter found Moses and raised him as her own. As an adult, Moses had a choice. He could live the life of royalty or turn his back on all of that luxury and fight for his people, the enslaved Hebrews. He chose the latter. Hebrews 11:24–25 tells us,

> By faith Moses, when he had grown up, refused to be known as the son of the Pharaoh's daughter. He chose to be mistreated along with the people of God rather than to enjoy the pleasures of sin for a short time.

Moses was honest about his heritage and who God had created him to be. He chose to exchange luxury and power for a life of service to God. His allegiance to God and the Hebrew people was stronger than his desire for personal power and wealth.

The fundamental issue that determines the extent to which God can bless your leadership is your heart.

I've been in ministry my whole life. I have never had lots of money, and that's probably a good thing. Every time we return from vacation, I tell my wife, Lisa, that I am designed to be independently wealthy. I just know I am! I'm meant to live on a beach and sip drinks with umbrellas in them. That's my calling, but somehow God hasn't seen it that way yet.

He seems to have a different purpose for me. And he has one for you too. "'For I know the plans I have for you,' declares the LORD, 'plans to prosper you and not to harm you, plans to give you hope and a future'" (Jer. 29:11). God has a unique plan for your life; and no one else on this earth can fulfill God's purpose for you. Each one of us has 168 hours in a week; and he wants you to use part of your 168 hours to influence the people in your small group.

When you understand your identity is in Jesus Christ (John 15) and not in the labels you wear, the emblems on your car, the zip code or neighborhood you live in, the vacations you take, the salary you receive, the color of your skin, or the church you work at, then you are able to answer this first question and move to the second.

2. Priority: What Is Really Most Important?

When Moses gave up living the life of royalty, it was not because he knew his life as a leader would be one of importance. He had no idea of the path ahead. He did know, however, that the life of an Israelite did not compare to the life of an Egyptian, let alone Egyptian royalty. His people, the Israelites, lived as slaves. To side with them would bring disgrace on his life in the eyes of many. Hebrews 11:26 tells us, "He regarded disgrace for the sake of Christ as of greater value than the treasures of Egypt, because he was looking ahead to his reward."

Personal disgrace for the sake of Christ was reasonable to Moses because serving God was a priority in his life. Moses knew how to accept suffering. And there will be some suffering for Christians because being a Christian does not mean that you get a "get out of jail free" card.

I understand what it is like to suffer. My son, Ethan, is autistic, and it is a lifelong struggle. My wife, Lisa, and I don't know if he will ever be able to live on his own. If I dwell on that, it can crush me. God is not sitting up in heaven going, "Whew! Man . . . what happened down there? That caught me by surprise!" God is not surprised at what's going on in my life, and he is not surprised by what is going on in your life. He is using all of the circumstances of our lives to shape and mold us. He is not concerned about *equity* for all in this life but about *eternity* for all in the next life.

Moses had the ability to look at the big picture. He lived in light of eternity and looked ahead to his reward. As a small group leader, you need to develop that same ability. The choices you make will reflect your character and the state of your heart, and that will determine how much God is able to use you. God is not concerned as much with your comfort as he is with your character. Once you decide to follow Christ and surrender your life to him, you're in this for the long haul. People may disappoint you; they may misunderstand and criticize you. But regardless of hard circumstances and hard people, submit yourself to loving Christ, loving his people, and looking ahead to your promised reward. It's the people, not the things around us, who matter most in this life.

The wife of one of my friends was diagnosed with cancer this past year. Nine short months later, her young life ended. During those nine months a group of people got together and did an extreme makeover on their home. It was a very nice gesture. But in the end, it didn't matter. Remarking privately on how beautiful the home looked, she said that she appreciated their hard work, but she also said the beauty of the home really didn't matter. When it came down to it, what mattered were the people around her. So often our priorities are misplaced. We put *stuff* ahead of *souls*. If you understand your priorities, then press ahead to the third question.

3. Responsibility: What Will I Do with My Life?

Remember that this is God's small group, not yours. He is entrusting it to you as part of his plan for your life. Continually ask him, "God, what do you want to happen in this small group? What can I do to better serve you and the people you have entrusted to me?" If you are leading a small group, God believes that you have something to offer the people in that group. Read the exchange between Moses and God found in Exodus 3:9–11.

> "And now the cry of the Israelites has reached me, and I have seen the way the Egyptians are oppressing them. So now, go. I am sending you to Pharaoh to bring my people the Israelites out of Egypt."
>
> But Moses said to God, "Who am I, that I should go to Pharaoh and bring the Israelites out of Egypt?"

Sound familiar? It does to me. God asks me to do something and immediately I wonder, *Who am I that I should go?* It was no different with Moses. He had his doubts; he felt unqualified. But here is the key: Despite his own misgivings and feelings of inadequacy, he obeyed. Moses could have shrugged off his responsibility to the Israelites, but he made the choice to take on the responsibility of serving those people.

Look at it this way. God believes in you so much that he entrusted to you his most valuable possessions on this planet—people. He knows you are the right person to shepherd these souls along a journey that gets them closer to him and the purpose he has for their lives. Wow, think of it! God is trusting you! The question is, Will you accept that responsibility? Is that responsibility enough for you to change your life to align with the priority and identity he has set before you?

4. Perseverance: How Far Will I Go?

Moses was the model of perseverance. "By faith he left Egypt, not fearing the king's anger; he persevered because he saw him who is invisible" (Heb. 11:27). You will probably not be asked to leave your country and lead your small group around in the wilderness for forty years, but you *will* be tempted to give up leadership . . . many times. The key is to persevere when you want to quit. In order to do that, you must have faith. Faith and obedience are prerequisites for spiritual leadership.

Faith does not stop with the initial believing; you must persevere and obey through every stage of life, by faith. "So then, just as you received Christ Jesus as Lord, continue to live in him, rooted and built up in him, strengthened in the faith as you were taught, and overflowing with thankfulness" (Col. 2:6–7).

Perseverance is a function of perspective; you will persevere to the end if you keep in mind who Christ is (the vine), and who you are (a branch).

Perseverance is a function of perspective; you will persevere to the end if you keep in mind who Christ is (the vine), and who you are (a branch). "I am the vine; you are the branches. If a man remains in me and I in him, he will bear much fruit; apart from me you can do nothing" (John 15:5). Baptism is not about getting wet; it's about being obedient. Tithing is not about money; it's about being obedient. Fasting isn't about being without food; it's about being obedient. Surrendering something, whether it is money, food, or your time, is not about the thing you are sacrificing. It is a question of obedience. How far are you willing to go to be obedient to God?

How to Lead Your Group: Three Essentials

Throughout my years of ministry, three traits stand out in leaders who lead groups well. They lead in these ways.

With Heart

Above all else, you need to connect to your small group with your heart. Jesus often used the example of a shepherd tending a flock. "I am the good shepherd; I know my sheep and my sheep know me" (John 10:14). While it may be a bit more difficult to relate to the example of a shepherd caring for a flock of sheep in our modern world, the principle is still the same. As a small group leader, you must know the individuals in your group (your flock), and they must know you. The only way that will happen is if you lead with your heart and show that you care for them like you care for yourself. When you do that and show your heart is in the group, your members will follow.

With Compassion

The first Scripture verse most of us memorized is John 11:35, "Jesus wept." Why did Jesus cry? Because his friend Lazarus had died. Jesus is recorded as crying one other place in the New Testament. "As he approached Jerusalem and saw the city, he wept over it" (Luke 19:41). Your ministry must be carried out with this same compassion. As Jesus came closer to Jerusalem, he saw the city ahead and he began to weep. Luke describes Jesus looking down on Jerusalem and seeing all of the lost people—sheep without a shepherd. This sight brings tears to the eyes of Christ. He had compassion for the people he was serving. How do you see the people of your church? Of your greater community? Of the world at large?

In Matthew 9:36 we get another glimpse into the character of Christ. "When he saw the crowds, he had compassion on them, because they were harassed and helpless, like sheep without a shepherd." Christ does not want us to forget what drew him to such compassion. He didn't weep over buildings, fancy programs, or other material things; he felt compassion for people. Without a leader, we are harassed, helpless, and defenseless as sheep. During the tough times, will you see your group members as impositions, or will you see them with compassion, as Jesus did?

With Motivation

In 2 Corinthians 5:10 we are told that at the end of time "we must all appear before the judgment seat of Christ." There are two judgments at the end of time: (1) Unbelievers are judged at the great white throne. They are cast into an eternity without God or without Christ, which is the purest form of hell. (2) Believers will be judged at the judgment seat of Christ. We will be asked two questions: "Did you know my Son, Jesus Christ?" And you will say yes! You wouldn't be there unless you had accepted Christ. The second question he is going to ask is, "What did you do with what I gave you?" Specific to your small group—he is entrusting their care to you. At the end time I want to hear him say, "Well done, good and faithful servant" (Matt. 25:21). That is my motivation. I pray it is yours.

ACTION STEPS

1. What are the three things this chapter stirred up in you?

2. What needs to change in your life based on this chapter?

3. What one thing can you do today to honor God in your daily life?

2

Your Role in God's Plan

Giving Your Group Purpose

Day after day, in the temple courts and from house to house, they never stopped teaching and proclaiming the good news that Jesus is the Christ.

Acts 5:42

Respect your fellow human being, treat them fairly, disagree with them honestly, enjoy their friendship, explore your thoughts about one another candidly, work together for a common goal and help one another achieve it.

Bill Bradley

Small groups were foundational to the early church. As you examine what the first home groups did, you can begin to develop a plan for your own small group.

Biblical Role Model

The Bible tells us that the small groups in New Testament times pursued the biblical purposes of fellowship, discipleship, ministry, evangelism, and worship. It was true then and it's true now that a healthy group will be focused on balancing those purposes.

> They devoted themselves to the apostles' teaching and to fellowship, to the breaking of bread and to prayer. Everyone was filled with awe at the many wonders and signs performed by the apostles. All the believers were together and had everything in common. They sold property and possessions to give to anyone who had need. Every day they continued to meet together in the temple courts. They broke bread in their homes and ate together with glad and sincere hearts, praising God and enjoying the favor of all the people. And the Lord added to their number daily those who were being saved. (Acts 2:42–47 TNIV)

The small groups that met in homes, as recorded in the book of Acts, were a strategic part of the greater church, just as your small group is a strategic part of your church.

1. *Fellowship*: "They joined in the fellowship . . . and ate together with glad and sincere hearts." That's important in the body of Christ—recognizing that I am a part of God's family and we are going to fellowship together. When you look at the New Testament, this is exactly what Christ did. He gathered a group of twelve guys and hung out with them. They ate together, learned together, and shared in each other's lives. Not only will true fellowship connect you and your members to each other, but it will also connect all of you to Christ.
2. *Discipleship*: The Bible says, "They devoted themselves to the apostles' teaching." That means they devoted themselves to growing in Christ and maturity. Evidently

they not only listened to what the disciples were teaching in the temple courts (equivalent to our *church*) on the Sabbath and other days but also gathered in their homes and studied together what they had been taught in the temple courts. Doing a Bible study is just one piece of discipleship. It's not only *learning* about the Word of God but also bringing its truth into every aspect of our lives. It is about helping each other identify and take our spiritual next step.

3. *Ministry*: They gave "to anyone who had need." These groups became an outlet of support for each other and for other members of the church. Your small group needs to be more than just a meeting that happens on a Tuesday night. Your members need to be engaged in ministry, which is simply meeting the needs of people within your church (as well as within your small group). *Ministry* is another word for *service*—serving one another in practical ways. Sometimes the ministry will take place right in your groups as people walk through a crisis together. Or it may be something as simple as giving a group member a ride to the airport or getting together as a group and painting a room in the church. This often leads to members discovering how God has gifted them in a way that is perfectly suited for service in your church.

4. *Evangelism*: That was their mission. *Ministry* is a way of serving other believers. *Mission* is serving the world (and unbelievers) at large. "And the Lord added to their number daily those who were being saved." Your group also should have a mission to the world and a ministry to the church. That world includes your neighborhood, your community, and the rest of the world. It can start as simply praying for your neighbors and could then progress to planning activities designed for building bridges with those who are not followers of Christ. People are attracted to the changes they see taking place

in the lives of healthy Christians. Your group can serve as a magnet for drawing people to Christ. Every small group has the potential to participate in and contribute to personal, local, and global missions.

5. *Worship*: "They devoted themselves . . . to the breaking of bread and to prayer. . . . [They were] praising God." These early Christians worshiped in their homes. And what was the result? "Everyone was filled with awe at the many wonders and signs performed by the apostles." Worship is not just the music we experience during the weekend service. Worship is about surrendering your life to Christ so you can live more abundantly and become more like Christ in nature. Small groups help members become more transparent as they receive the support they need to flourish in their Christian walk. This increased transparency provides the fertile ground for worship.

Define Success Clearly

Unless you know what the target is, you cannot hit it. For Saddleback Church, *success* is a church full of healthy followers of Christ. We determined that healthy followers of Christ are people who are balancing the five biblical purposes in their life and in their heart.

They are:

experiencing healthy relationships with other people (fellowship)

growing in Christ both cognitively and experientially (discipleship)

discovering and using their God-given gifts and abilities (ministry)

reaching out and sharing the love of Christ with unbelievers (evangelism) surrendering their heart and life to Christ on an ongoing basis (worship)

Our target is health as expressed through balancing those five biblical purposes. The way we get there is through our small groups.

Know Your Vision and Mission

What is the purpose of your church? Does your church have a vision and mission statement? Do you know it? Do the members of your small group know it? If not, you need to start there.

Your small group is a reflection of your church. As such, group members should also reflect the purpose of the church. The very best way to get the people of the church in alignment with the vision and mission of your church is by repeated exposure. In order to accomplish this, your small group must be in alignment with the church. The idea is for everyone to be moving in the same direction—toward a healthy and balanced life centered on Christ.

The purpose statement of Saddleback Church is:

To bring people to Jesus and membership in his family, develop them to Christlike maturity, and equip them for their ministry in the church and life mission in the world, in order to magnify God's name.

The vision and mission statements of Saddleback's small group ministry are:

Vision: to see every person, from the core of our church, to the ever-growing community, connected in a healthy small group.

Mission: to help spiritual seekers become transformed believers who model purpose driven lives and motivate others to do the same.

Our small group ministry vision and mission statements are both in alignment with the purpose statement of the church. Everything we do in our small groups falls under those two statements.

Know Your Role

Your role as a small group leader is not one of a teacher or sage: "I am up here and you are down there." Teaching is often too passive and misses the power of the relational connection. Small group leaders need to involve themselves in the lives of other people just as Christ did. Leaders also need to allow group members to be involved in their life. Ideally, all group members will be helping each other to grow and take spiritual next steps because they will be more than members of the same group—they will be friends. Your role as the leader is to build that expectation into your group and then encourage the fulfillment of it.

Small group leaders need to involve themselves in the lives of other people just as Christ did.

Balance of the Purposes Is Key

When we first started trying to balance the purposes in the small groups, we tried to get them to balance all of the purposes in every meeting. We suggested that they start with fifteen minutes of fellowship, move on to fifteen minutes of discipleship, and so on. We even had our small group studies divided up accordingly to make it easier for them. We thought that was a great idea. It was not. It failed miserably.

45

We found that the groups were so busy trying to balance all of the purposes that they couldn't finish the curriculum. The principle was right, but the methodology was wrong.

Now, we still want all of our groups to balance the purposes but it is not about doing every purpose at every meeting. Instead, over the course of six months you can evaluate your group according to how much time overall you spend on each purpose. To aid in this evaluation, we provide our groups with a tool called the Group Health Plan. This will be discussed in more detail in chapter 3, but for now, just begin to think about balancing the purposes over a period of time—such as six months or a year. At the end of the time period, your group can take an evening to assess how the group is doing in balancing the purposes. At that point you can make adjustments and work on the purpose(s) that need strengthening.

Groups naturally gravitate toward fellowship. We're wired that way. My group is the same. I am more of a fellowship person. If my group got together for three hours and just fellowshipped, I would be euphoric. But that would not bring health and balance to the group. As the leader, you need to be aware of your natural tendency to favor the purpose you feel most comfortable with and counteract that by empowering the people in your group who are strong in the other purposes through continual assessment and encouragement.

It is actually quite easy to balance the purposes with a little intention and focus. We give our small groups a book entitled *250 Big Ideas for Purpose Driven Small Groups*, which provides fifty practical and fun ideas for each purpose. Another tool we provide is an audio series called "Don't Lead Alone." It teaches the leader how to give the ministry away and build a healthy group that balances the five biblical purposes. You can get these tools at www.smallgroups. net/store.

Small Group Guidelines

We also provide each of our small groups with a printed copy of our small group guidelines so they are all on the same page from the very first meeting. If your church does not supply a guideline, you may want to ask the person in your church who is responsible for small groups to think about creating one. The guidelines we use at Saddleback can be found at www.smallgroups.net/gg. Feel free to edit it for your own use. Small group guidelines typically cover things such as purpose of the group, frequency of meetings, and attendance.

As you lead your small group, keep in mind the following basic facilitation tips so you can bring out the best of each person in your group.

1. *Don't do all of the talking.* Strive to facilitate the conversation and keep it moving from member to member rather than talking *to* the members and they merely answer. See the two diagrams in figure 2.1. One is of a leader dispensing information; the other is of a leader facilitating conversation. Note how the flow of the latter conversation involves all group members. Ideas and information are bounced off from member to member, not merely fed back to the leader.

Figure 2.1
Dispensing/Facilitating

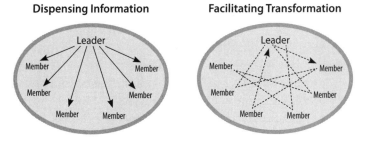

Dispensing Information

Facilitating Transformation

2. *Be comfortable with silence.* Fifteen seconds of silence in group life can seem like an eternity—especially when you are the leader. But realize that when you have silence, the Holy Spirit is working on people. When you interrupt the silence, you interrupt the Holy Spirit. Be willing to sit in silence as people process the information that is being shared. We are so programmed for business that silence can seem wrong, when in fact, it can be the best thing for your group.

3. *Be a good listener.* One evening Lisa was talking to me while I was sort of listening. We were having a discussion (she was talking while I was doing some head nodding and answering a couple of emails on my laptop). Very shortly into *our* conversation, she looked at me and said, "Tell me what I just said."

My dark side kicked in and I said, "Well if you really want to know, you just asked me the question, 'What did I just say?'" That didn't go over too well; I would not recommend it as a way to build your relationship.

How many times have you been on your cell with somebody and checking email on the computer at the same time? I've heard people do that to me because I can hear the clicking of their keyboard over the phone. So I am going to put a stop to this. I am looking for a quiet keyboard that doesn't click. Okay—just kidding.

James 1:19 tells us to be slow to speak and quick to listen. That is advice we could all benefit from, especially as leaders. Learn to listen with your eyes as well as your ears.

4. *Don't answer your own questions.* Of course you know the answer, but the whole purpose of asking a question is to let the group members discuss the answer. Get comfortable with silence. If a full minute has passed and no one has answered, you may want to share something just to encourage members to open up. Maybe say, "Tom, you look like you were going to say something. . . ."

5. *Ask open-ended questions.* Open-ended questions prompt members to answer with more than a simple yes or no. Do not ask, "Did you like this chapter of the book?" Instead ask, "What did you like or dislike about this chapter of the book?" Use *what* or *how* questions to get people to open up.

6. *Begin and end on time.* If your group time is supposed to end at 8:00 pm, be sure to have someone watch the clock. At 8:00 pm tell everyone the group is officially over but if they want to stay and chat for a few minutes, they may. You need to respect everyone's time because some members will need to get up early the next morning, or others may have to pick up the kids at the babysitter's house. For this reason, always begin and end group at the agreed-upon time. What is interesting is that many times, most people stay and continue to chat afterward. Sometimes the best group meeting is the meeting after the formal meeting. You can take that to the bank!

Your job as the leader of the group is to continually cast vision.

7. *Have a small group guideline.* Renew it yearly or whenever you add a new person to the group. (See chapters 2, 4, and 15.)

8. *Make sure everyone understands the purpose of the group from day one.* Your job as the leader of the group is to continually cast vision. Keep that purpose before the group and look for ways to promote vision casting in every meeting.

9. *Try to involve everyone.* Do you want to know if your group is too big? See if each person gets a chance to talk. If they don't, your group is too big and you need to subdivide. Be sure that everyone gets a chance to speak and share. Groups of over eight members will have difficulty doing this. In those cases, it is best to divide the group in half; perhaps beginning together to watch a video and

then moving into two groups for the discussion questions. (See chapter 11 for more on subgrouping.)

10. *Remember, the focus is not on getting through the material.* The purpose is people development. If you are very task oriented, you may tend to concentrate more on getting through the study than allowing group members the time they need to discuss, process, and grow with the information.

11. *Make sure all cell phones are turned off.* Do not use cell phones during group meetings (and yes, that includes sending text messages). Make it a rule that cell phones are put on vibrate before the group starts. You may want to model that behavior by pulling out your cell phone in front of group members, turning it on vibrate, and saying something like, "Time to turn the cell phones to vibrate." Of course those who have their kids with a babysitter will want to keep their cell phone close.

12. *Ask for help.* Partner with your spouse or another individual (same sex) in your group for prayer support as well as for practical assistance in administration, hospitality, and accountability. This is critical and will be discussed more in chapter 9.

13. *Be prepared.* Always read the assigned reading or review the DVD session and familiarize yourself with the questions before the group arrives. If any questions of your own come up, be sure to jot them down. Never be afraid to say, "I don't know the answer to that question. But I'm sure over the past two thousand years someone has answered it, and I'll find the answer before next week."

14. *Pray.* Pray before your group meeting. Pray after your group meeting. Pray during group meetings (yup, if an appropriate moment comes up, stop and pray right then). Pray in between group meetings. Ask God for his help and leading. Pray for group members by name.

If it is helpful, make a list of their prayer requests and keep them on a bedside table so you can be very specific in your prayer requests.

15. *Remember that God is in charge.* You were not selected to lead this group on your own. If God chose you, he will be with you. Trust in that and lean on him for support. Be open to his leading and always seek his will.

The most effective leaders have four key relationships in their life. No matter where you are in your journey as a leader, I encourage you to develop these key relationships.

1. *You need a relationship with Christ.* If you do not have a relationship with Christ, nothing you do as a leader will have much of an impact. You do not need to be a *perfect* Christian (there is no such thing), but you do need to be surrendering your life to Christ and asking for his guidance on a continual basis.

2. *You need someone who is one level ahead of you.* Depending on how your small group ministry is set up, this may be a more experienced small group leader, a community leader or coach, or in the case of a smaller church, your pastor, director of small groups, or small group point person. You need to be able to go to someone for advice, support, and encouragement.

3. *You need a spiritual partner.* A spiritual partner is somebody who knows your issues. He or she provides accountability and support in the areas of life you're working on.

4. *You need an apprentice.* Each one of us needs to have somebody we're pouring our lives into. Just as you look for people with more experience to guide you, you need to be guiding someone else within your group. If you had to move out of town tomorrow, who would be the most likely person to take your place? Even if you never move, you need someone who can take over the

The enemy likes us to operate in isolation. Jesus operates in community. group when you are on vacation or ill. Beyond the practical nature of having an apprentice, it is your duty as a leader to be developing other leaders. The enemy likes us to operate in isolation. Jesus operates in community. Whenever he sent out the disciples, he always sent them out in pairs. Be thinking about developing an apprentice. We will be discussing this more in later chapters, but for now, if you don't have an apprentice, start praying about who in your group that may be. What's cool is that the apprentice doesn't even have to know he or she is a future leader.

Why are these four relationships vital to your success? The enemy wants you to function in isolation; God wants you to function in a supportive community. Don't make the mistake of trying to go it alone. To do so sets you up for failure. Be strategic and don't allow your strengths to fool you into thinking you don't need these relationships.

ACTION STEPS

1. Respond to the following questions regarding the four relationships in your life.

   a. How is your relationship with Christ?

   _____

   _____

   _____

   b. Who is your *one level ahead* relationship?

   _____

   _____

   _____

c. Who is your spiritual partner?

d. Who is your apprentice?

2. If you are missing any of the relationships above, who can fulfill that role for you? Contact that person today.

3. What is the purpose of your small group?

4. Is your group fulfilling that purpose? If not, what is one step you can take this week to move toward that goal?

3

It Starts with You

Your Plan and Your Group's Plan

Test yourselves to make sure you are solid in the faith. Don't drift along taking everything for granted. Give yourselves regular checkups. You need firsthand evidence, not mere hearsay, that Jesus Christ is in you. Test it out. If you fail the test, do something about it.

2 Corinthians 13:5 Message

A leader leads by example, whether he intends to or not.

Anonymous

What does spiritual health look like? Some measure spiritual health by having the right answers to theological questions. Others believe spiritual health is demonstrated by acts of service. While these are good things, our spiritual life suffers if we do not balance all five of God's purposes in our lives.

Spiritual Health Assessment and Plan

To help group members evaluate their lives in light of the five biblical purposes, we have developed a Spiritual Health Assessment. Like our physical health, our spiritual health needs to be assessed and managed. The Spiritual Health Assessment will help group members rate themselves through a series of statements designed to get at the heart issues behind each of the purposes.

It is important for your group members to understand that this assessment is simply a starting point and is not intended to cover every area of their life and faith. It does, however, provide a way for them to begin thinking about how they can bring health and balance to their lives.

Over the years I have taken many tests and assessments, and I have found them to be too detailed with too many questions, which can cause people to become overwhelmed. But an assessment doesn't need to be complex; it just needs to move people toward action and spiritual health. That is what we have attempted to do in this assessment.

The assessment will provide a snapshot of how well they are balancing the purposes in their lives and will enable them to identify areas in which they may need to pursue further growth. It will also benefit the group as a whole because it will reveal areas in which they have a strength they can share with others who may need help in that area.

In order to help group members assess their strong areas and how to develop a plan for improvement, we put together two tools that we offer in a single booklet (available at www.smallgroups.net/store.

Spiritual Health Assessment. This self-assessment tool (shown in table 3.1) is designed to help people take a snapshot of their life and see how well they are balancing the five biblical purposes. The goal is neither to score high nor to compare themselves with others. Rather, it provides a starting point from which people can begin to pursue a healthier spiritual life.

Spiritual Health Plan. Once they have completed the Spiritual Health Assessment and have identified a weak area, this tool helps them develop an action plan for growing in that area (see table 3.2).

The assessment is divided into the five biblical purposes, and is designed to answer the following questions:

Healthy Fellowship: How are you doing in the area of community?

Healthy Discipleship: What is your spiritual next step?

Healthy Ministry: How are you gifted?

Healthy Evangelism: Who do you plan to take to heaven with you?

Healthy Worship: What do you need to surrender?

When using the Spiritual Health Plan to write down goals you feel the Lord wants you to work toward, think in developmental steps, which I call the crawl, walk, run framework (see figure 3.1). The first year I did the Spiritual Health Assessment, I gave my best shot at the Spiritual Health Plan. The tool was still in the development stage, and we were testing it to determine what worked and what didn't. At that time we did not have crawl, walk, and run steps, and I soon found my goals were too high, so I couldn't see progress in the first month. Discouraged, I procrastinated on the very goals I felt the Lord wanted me to grow toward. So through the process of developing my own Spiritual Health Plan and failing to achieve my goals, I decided to create a crawl, walk, run version of those goals. Doing so helped me see progress as I conquered small, attainable steps along the way.

Table 3.1

Spiritual Health Assessment

Worship: You Were Planned for God's Pleasure	Doesn't Describe Me		Partially Describes Me		Generally Describes Me
How I live my life shows that God is my highest priority.	1	2	3	4	5
I am dependent on God for every aspect of my life.	1	2	3	4	5
There is nothing in my life that I have not surrendered to (have kept back from) God.	1	2	3	4	5
I regularly meditate on God's Word and invite him into my everyday activities.	1	2	3	4	5
I have a deep desire to spend time in God's presence.	1	2	3	4	5
I am the same person in public that I am in private.	1	2	3	4	5
I have an overwhelming sense of God's awesomeness even when I do not feel his presence.	1	2	3	4	5
			Worship Total _____		

Fellowship: You Were Formed for God's Family	Doesn't Describe Me		Partially Describes Me		Generally Describes Me
I am genuinely open and honest about who I am.	1	2	3	4	5
I regularly use my time and resources to care for the needs of others.	1	2	3	4	5
I have a deep and meaningful connection with others in the church.	1	2	3	4	5
I have an easy time receiving advice, encouragement, and correction from others.	1	2	3	4	5
I gather regularly with a group of Christians for fellowship and accountability.	1	2	3	4	5

Fellowship: You Were Formed for God's Family	Doesn't Describe Me		Partially Describes Me		Generally Describes Me
There is nothing in my relationships that is currently unresolved.	1	2	3	4	5
There is nothing in the way I talk or act concerning others that I would not be willing to share with them in person.	1	2	3	4	5

Fellowship Total _____

Discipleship: You Were Created to Become Like Christ	Doesn't Describe Me		Partially Describes Me		Generally Describes Me
I am quick to confess anything in my character that does not look like Christ.	1	2	3	4	5
A review of how I use my finances shows that I think more about God and others than I do about myself.	1	2	3	4	5
I allow God's Word to guide my thoughts and change my actions.	1	2	3	4	5
I am able to praise God during difficult times and see them as opportunities to grow.	1	2	3	4	5
I find I am making better choices to do what is right when I am tempted to do wrong.	1	2	3	4	5
I have found that prayer has changed how I view and interact with the world.	1	2	3	4	5
I am consistent in pursuing habits that are helping me model my life after Jesus.	1	2	3	4	5

Discipleship Total _____

Ministry: You Were Shaped for Serving God	Doesn't Describe Me		Partially Describes Me		Generally Describes Me
I regularly use my time to serve God.	1	2	3	4	5
I am currently serving God with the gifts and passions he has given me.	1	2	3	4	5
I regularly reflect on how my life can have an impact for the kingdom of God.	1	2	3	4	5
I often think about ways to use my God-given gifts and abilities to please God.	1	2	3	4	5
I enjoy meeting the needs of others without expecting anything in return.	1	2	3	4	5
Those closest to me would say my life is a reflection of giving more than receiving.	1	2	3	4	5
I see my painful experiences as opportunities to minister to others.	1	2	3	4	5

Ministry Total _____

Evangelism: You Were Made for a Mission	Doesn't Describe Me		Partially Describes Me		Generally Describes Me
I feel personal responsibility to share my faith with those who don't know Jesus.	1	2	3	4	5
I look for opportunities to build relationships with those who don't know Jesus.	1	2	3	4	5
I regularly pray for those who don't know Christ.	1	2	3	4	5
I am confident in my ability to share my faith.	1	2	3	4	5
My heart is full of passion to share the Good News of the gospel with those who have never heard it.	1	2	3	4	5

Evangelism: You Were Made for a Mission	Doesn't Describe Me		Partially Describes Me		Generally Describes Me
I find that my relationship with Jesus comes up frequently in my conversations with those who don't know him.	1	2	3	4	5
I am open to going anywhere God calls me, in whatever capacity, to share my faith.	1	2	3	4	5
			Evangelism Total		_____

Transfer your scores to the Spiritual Health Plan.

It is not difficult to use these tools by following these seven steps:

1. *Before you begin to take the Spiritual Health Assessment, pray!* Pray for an open mind to how the Holy Spirit wants to use this assessment in your life. This is not a test you take one time and then move on to something else. It is a living document that starts with the Spiritual Health Assessment and then provides accountability in the Spiritual Health Plan. As D. L. Moody said, "Discipleship is not in the information, but the transformation."

2. *Take the Spiritual Health Assessment.* This assessment (shown in table 3.1) is divided into five sections: worship, fellowship, discipleship, ministry, and evangelism. In each of the sections there are seven statements pertaining to that area, for a total of thirty-five statements. For each statement, score yourself from 1 to 5, with 1 indicating "doesn't describe me" and 5 indicating "generally describes me." For example, the first statement in the area of worship is: "How I live my life shows that God is my highest priority." After reading the statement, the test-taker circles the appropriate

Pray for an open mind to how the Holy Spirit wants to use this assessment in your life.

60

score. When all the statements are marked, add up the scores under each purpose. Let's say you end up with the following scores:

Worship: 16
Fellowship: 20
Discipleship: 24
Ministry: 19
Evangelism: 18

These scores indicate that worship is an area in which you will want to grow, while discipleship is an area in which you can contribute to your small group.

Table 3.2

Spiritual Health Plan for _____ **(your name)**

I will share my plan with _____, who will be my spiritual partner to help me balance the five biblical purposes in my life.

Purposes	Practices	Partnership	Progress
What purposes are out of balance?	*What do I need to do, and when?*	*Who will help me in this purpose?*	*What progress have I made?*
Worship How I scored myself ____ How my friend scored me ____			
Fellowship How I scored myself ____ How my friend scored me ____			
Discipleship How I scored myself ____ How my friend scored me ____			

Purposes	Practices	Partnership	Progress
Ministry How I scored myself _____ How my friend scored me _____			
Evangelism How I scored myself _____ How my friend scored me _____			

3. *Find the purpose(s) you want to work on.* In our example above, you would want to work on the area of worship.

4. *Choose a crawl, walk, or run step to get started.* Inside the same booklet that holds the Spiritual Health Assessment and the Spiritual Health Plan is a list of crawl, walk, run steps for each purpose. These suggestions correlate with every question in the Spiritual Health Assessment. For example, let's say you scored 2 on the first worship statement: "How I live my life shows that God is my highest priority." Turning to the crawl, walk, run suggestions for worship, you find the recommended steps for that question:

> *Crawl:* Ask a friend or spouse to help you identify your top priorities. What changes do you need to make?
>
> *Walk:* Spend time reading through the life stories of some of the people in the Old Testament. Journal about the characteristics in their lives that demonstrate that God was a priority. What principles can you implement in your own life?
>
> *Run:* Make it a habit each evening to reflect on your activities for that day. Journal or spend time in prayer over how you saw God in your daily activities. How are your priorities shaped by recognition of God's presence?

Figure 3.1
Crawl to Run

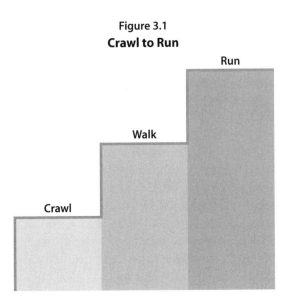

5. *Transfer the steps to your Spiritual Health Plan.* The plan shown in table 3.2 is a tool for you to write down the goals you feel the Lord wants you to work toward. As you do this, think in the crawl, walk, or run step framework for each purpose (or just the one purpose on which you scored the lowest). Start slow and develop a plan that will work for you. Make sure you have a *what* and a *when* in the Practices column; this helps your goal be measurable and specific.

6. *Share your Spiritual Health Plan with a few trusted people.* Notice that in the Partnership column you can select people you want to ask to help you with this particular step. If no one knows what you have on your plan, it's easy to procrastinate. The devil seeks to defeat our plans by isolating us, but the loving community around us keeps us on track toward our goals. So fill out your Spiritual Health Plan and then show it to some people in your small group whom you trust or your spiritual partner. Taking it a step further, you may

want to encourage your spiritual partner to also take the Spiritual Health Assessment and come up with his or her own Spiritual Health Plan for the year. Then the two of you can provide support, encouragement, and accountability for each other.

7. *Keep track of your progress throughout the year.* This can be recorded in the Progress column of the health plan, and it will document whether you hit your target goal of the *when*. The people with whom you shared your Spiritual Health Plan can help you check up on the entire plan throughout the year. Since the health plan is a living document, it will change throughout the year. The plans you set in January may look completely different in July. That's okay because as God works in your life there *will* be changes.

Another feature of this tool is the Friend Feedback Assessment. This is exactly the same as the Spiritual Health Assessment except it provides the perspective of another person. For example, you give the Friend Feedback Assessment to your friend and ask him or her to score you on the statements under the five biblical purposes. It is often enlightening to discover how others feel we are doing in our spiritual walk.

Fresh Start

On the first Friday of every year, Lisa and I take some time alone and share our personal Spiritual Health Plans for the coming year. In 1999, when my daughter, Erika, was just a baby, Lisa and I hired a sitter and went out and exchanged our plans over dessert. I looked hers over quickly and said, "This looks good," and handed it back to her. She held mine in her hands and was still reading. I waited for her response. A few long minutes passed, and eventually she said, "I think there are some things that you're missing that are holes in your spiritual life, and you should probably write them down here." So I said, "Oh? Can I have your planner back? Because I'm ready to be honest too." I can play this game!

As our conversation continued, one of the things she suggested I add to my planner was "develop family time." That is because a number of years before, I almost made a train wreck of our marriage. I fell more in love with my work than I was with my wife. We didn't have children at the time, and we were able to work through it with some counseling. Since we had recently added a baby to the picture, Lisa wanted to make sure I did not fall back into my old ways of being a workaholic. So I added "develop family time" to my Spiritual Health Plan, and we finished dessert.

A few months later, I was involved in a two-day conference at Saddleback. As I walked in the back door at the end of the first day, Lisa asked, "Hey, can you change Erika's diaper?" I barely broke stride and quickly replied, "Sure, babe. I just want to download a couple of thoughts from the conference first. I'll just go upstairs really quick and do that, and I promise you that in five minutes I'll be back down to change her diaper."

Without a word, she walked over to the counter where my Spiritual Health Plan was and pulled it out. She opened it deliberately, pointed to a page, and said, "Two months ago you vowed to me that you would work on this area. Your daughter is not an interruption in your busy schedule. If you want to be the spiritual head of this house and value your family, then you need to make a choice. Do you want to go upstairs or do you want to change her diaper?"

I felt like a sledgehammer had hit my chest. I mean, the wind was knocked out of me. I will never forget it.

I share this story at our Purpose Driven Small Group Conferences, and every time I tell it I have to choke back the tears. It still kills me.

Needless to say, I changed my daughter's diaper.

Applying the Assessment to Group Health

The Spiritual Health Assessment is a great tool designed for individual evaluation and health, and it can also be used as a small group tool to determine the overall health and balance of a group. Encourage your group members to take individual Spiritual Health Assessments and develop Personal Spiritual Health Plans. Once they have all scored themselves, suggest they get together to discuss how the group as a whole is doing in the area of balancing the purposes. Small groups can use the Group Health Plan (figure 3.2) to develop a snapshot of where their group is and then use the suggestions in tables 3.3 through 3.7 to develop crawl, walk, and run group opportunities for the five purposes.

First, use the top part of the Group Health Plan to write the names of the group members on the diamond according to where they scored high on the Spiritual Health Assessment. Later these names will be transferred over to the third column under "Who Will Help?" After that, have the group work on the first column: "What Are We Doing Currently?" Go through each purpose and have them write what they feel is currently being done in the group. They may write something or they may write nothing. That's okay; it's only a snapshot of where your group is now.

Next, use tables 3.3 through 3.7 to dream about ideas your group could do under "What Are Our Next Steps?" These should be goals your group could accomplish in the next six months. (The Group Health Plan is found in the Small Group Leader Training Kit at www.smallgroups.net/grouphealthplan.)

Once groups have a snapshot, they can use tables 3.3 through 3.7 for suggestions of crawl, walk, and run group opportunities for the five purposes. Encourage your group to think out of the box and perhaps even involve other groups in developing their spiritual next steps.

We have discovered many benefits from small groups using our assessment tools. They include:

1. *It can give your pastor insight into how to lead the congregation effectively.* For example, if most of your congregation is struggling with evangelism, the pastor could do a message series on evangelism or offer a class about how to share Jesus with others. The assessment allows you to look at levels of issues that go a little deeper than what most people talk about.

2. *It promotes a sense of shared responsibility for spiritual health.* Offering an assessment reminds people that spiritual health is up to each of us—it's not the pastor's responsibility. The group score is an aggregate so that people don't compare each other, and it encourages them to see that they're not alone when it comes to spiritual growth.

   Offering an assessment reminds people that spiritual health is up to each of us—it's not the pastor's responsibility.

3. *It gives people an intentional pathway for crawl, walk, and run steps.* The tool offers practical next steps for each of the purposes. For instance, if people score low in discipleship, there are suggestions for how they can build spiritual muscle in that area. This helps them plug into resources in the church and gets them thinking about movement, not arrival.

4. *It encourages people to serve out of their strengths.* By affirming people's strengths, it starts the process of organizing the church with intentionality. People mentor each other, and instead of focusing on weaknesses, accountability partners can share their strengths and learn from each other.

5. *It inspires us to set short-term goals.* We usually encourage people to take the assessment annually to check their progress and set short-term goals. It's a way to strengthen certain aspects of spiritual health over time.

6. *It helps grow healthy small groups.* This can be a great way for them to chart their spiritual health together. Again, the idea is not to look at individual scores but for group members to encourage each other and be accountable as they grow in Christ. When someone in the group shares that he or she struggles with evangelism and someone else says, "Me too," it's a moment for the whole group to learn and grow. If the group discovers that it is out of balance in that area, the members may decide to study a certain curriculum or try another crawl, walk, or run step.

It's about Health, Not Just a Connection

Your small group goal is health. We define success as balancing the biblical purposes. It is not about just connecting people because you can have 100 percent of your people in church connected in small groups, but if those groups are not spiritually healthy, you do not have a healthy small group ministry.

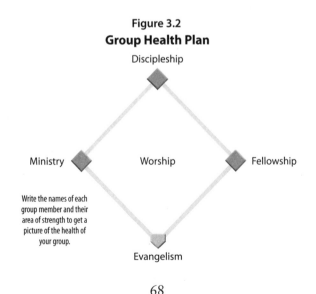

Figure 3.2
Group Health Plan

Discipleship

Ministry   Worship   Fellowship

Write the names of each group member and their area of strength to get a picture of the health of your group.

Evangelism

(Figure 3.2 con't.)
Moving toward Balance

Purpose	What Are We Doing Currently?	What Are Our Next Steps?	Who Will Help?
Worship			
Fellowship			
Discipleship			
Ministry			
Evangelism			

Table 3.3

Worship

Aspect of Worship	Crawl	Walk	Run
Prayer	Make it a point to pray for the group when you meet. You may want to open or close in prayer, but be sure you take the lead in making prayer a part of your group.	Have members of your group share specific things they need prayer for, and then pray for them. You may have one person pray for all the requests or have each member pray for one person. Be sure to keep a record of these prayers and ask about them on a weekly basis.	Take some time to lead your group through a time of structured prayer and meditation.
Singing Praise	Attend a worship service as a group and praise God together.	Invite someone to lead worship during your group time, or pick up worship DVDs from your local Christian bookstore.	Make singing and a time of praise a normal part of your small group meeting. You could sing a cappella, use the musical talents of members in your group who may play an instrument, or use a worship video/CD to help you worship together.
Communion Foot Washing	As a group, attend a worship service where communion is served. Spend some time in your next group meeting reflecting on how that time impacted each member.	Invite a leader from your church to your group to lead you in communion or a foot washing.	Lead your group or ask a group member to lead in a time of communion or foot washing. Make this a regular occurrence in your group.
Surrender	Get a study that focuses on ways to worship. What ways could you make this a practice in your group?	As a group, spend some time discussing things that each of you needs to surrender to God. Make it an open and confidential time of sharing your lives together. Commit to pray for those things that were shared. Spend some time taking communion together, remembering Christ's sacrifice of surrendering his life for you.	Agree as a group to fast together. It could be for one day or a specific time of day, and it could be from food or from something else. (Those with physical issues could fast from things other than food.) Spend the time together reflecting on your own dependence on God. Spend some time thanking God for all he has done for you and what he will do in the future.

Table 3.4

Fellowship

Aspect of Fellowship	Crawl	Walk	Run
Community Building	Celebrate significant occasions (birthdays, spiritual birthdays, etc.) as a group. Look for opportunities to play together.	Have an affirmation night where each person is in the "hot seat" while group members share what they appreciate about that person.	Go on a retreat together as a small group. This could be an affinity retreat (couples, singles, etc.) or a spiritual retreat. Carve out some time to be together.
Deepening Relationships	Make prayer a central part of how you deepen your relationship with one another. Have a regular time for sharing concerns and requests and write them down in a journal. Refer back to the journal frequently to see how God has answered your prayers.	Take a night in between studies to go to dinner and/or see a movie as a group. Look for opportunities to spend fun time together.	Plan a weekend trip or go to a camp together. Look for fun ways to share life together.
Meeting Needs	Take some time to pray for the needs of those in the group. You may want to write down those needs and check in with each other.	As people share their needs, look for ways that your group could rally around that person. There are some needs that we cannot meet, but make it a point to do everything you can to help each other.	Take the Spiritual Health Assessment as a group and discover each member's strengths. Then go through the Group Health Plan and have members meet some needs in your group based on those strengths.
Sharing Community	To remind you that you are open to sharing community with others, write down the name of someone with whom you would like to do lunch or have coffee.	Get to know other small groups in your community. You may want to have a get-together with another small group to share together.	Invite someone new into your group. You may know someone you can invite, or you could talk with the leaders of groups at your church about who is looking for a group in your area.

Table 3.5

Discipleship

Aspect of Discipleship	Crawl	Walk	Run
Curriculum	For your next series, spend time talking as a group about what the next topic of study should be. Have people share what their needs are and what they feel would be beneficial to study at this time. Then choose a topic.	For your next series, choose a topic that you have never considered as a group to stretch you and make your group more balanced. If you always study books of the Bible, try studying a topic related to life stages or spiritual habits. If you always do topical studies, try studying a book of the Bible. Have fun expanding your horizons.	Plan your curriculum or topic of study a year in advance. Try to move to a place where your curriculum is balanced. Make a goal to do at least one study on a book of the Bible (discipleship), one study related to life stages (fellowship), one study on spiritual health/disciplines (worship), and one study related to outreach (evangelism/ministry). Make your curriculum reflect the balance you want for your group.
Accountability	Have your group take the Spiritual Health Assessment. Ask each group member to share with one other person the area they have chosen to work on so they can pray for one another.	Take the Spiritual Health Assessment as a group. Have each person share their strength and the area they need to work on. You may want to have people pair up by gender based on strengths and weaknesses to mentor each other. (For example, if I am weak in evangelism, I should pair up with someone who is strong in evangelism.) Take the assessment on a regular basis (annually, biannually, etc.).	Have your group take the Spiritual Health Assessment and then walk through the Group Health Plan together. Look for ways to have group members take ownership of the group based on the strengths and passions they have for a particular purpose. Set goals for how you will balance the purposes over the next six months.
Spiritual Disciplines	Have each member of your group connect with another person in the group for prayer support. Have people share things they would like prayer for, and make it a point to have those pairs ask each other about their respective prayer requests regularly.	Have your group share with one another the struggles they have in their lives and one way the group can help them to grow. You may want to have the men in one room and the women in another to allow for open discussion. Pray for each other's needs and follow through on helping group members to grow.	Take the results from each person's Spiritual Health Assessment and, based on their strengths and weaknesses, match people up in the group by gender as spiritual partners. (For example, if I am weak in discipleship, I should pair up with someone who is strong in discipleship.) This will allow members of your group to build into each other's lives in a natural way and not be seen as taskmasters trying to hold to a plan. Share the results with the group from time to time.

Table 3.6

Ministry

Aspect of Ministry	Crawl	Walk	Run
Understanding Your S.H.A.P.E.	Do a study that explores how God has uniquely S.H.A.P.E.'d each person to serve. (See page 134 to learn more about your God-given S.H.A.P.E.)	Schedule some time to have someone from your church come to your group and share some of the ministry opportunities available based on the S.H.A.P.E. of your group members.	As a group, spend some time sharing each person's S.H.A.P.E. What are some ways that each member can contribute to owning the group, based on a particular purpose? Affirm and look for ways for them to contribute to the health of your group based on their passions for a particular purpose area.
Serving Your Group	Pick a way you can serve the members of your small group. You could wash a car for someone in your group, take care of the yard, or prepare a meal. Look for practical ways to serve each other.	Have each person in the group take on a role to help make the group better. Structure these roles around the purposes to help your group be balanced. Someone may want to handle the food (fellowship), handle prayer (worship), or trade off teaching (discipleship). Look for ways to include everyone so that each person can serve the group.	As a group, seek ways to serve other small groups. You may want to find out what the needs of another group are and try to meet them. Or you may want to offer to watch the children for a group so they can have a night out to build their fellowship together. Look for ways to connect with other groups in your area.
Serving Your Church as a Group	Take a night to serve the church by doing a simple project together, such as preparing a mailer to go out or preparing crafts for the children's ministry.	Take on a ministry event together as a group. You may want to volunteer to serve at one of the Easter or Christmas services.	Find a ministry that your group can support or serve in on a regular basis. Get a list of opportunities from your church and choose a way you can serve together as a group.
Serving Your Church with Your S.H.A.P.E.	Take some time as a group to reflect on the S.H.A.P.E. of each member. Have each person take turns being in the "hot seat," and have the rest of the group share the gifts and passions they see in that person. How could these gifts be expressed in ministry?	Have each person in your group take some time serving in one or two ministries in the church to get a feel for where they might best serve.	Encourage your group members to commit to serving in some kind of ministry at the church. Reflect regularly as a group about what God is doing in and through each person as they serve and celebrate God's goodness together.

Table 3.7

Evangelism

Aspect of Evangelism	Crawl	Walk	Run
Personal Evangelism	As a group, take a class on evangelism at your church. Spend some time discussing what you learned and how you could implement it in your group.	Identify three people whom you will pray for as a group, and make it a point to talk regularly about how you could invite them to your group.	Pick one person you will each share your faith with in the next week. Come back and report how it went. You may even want to invite the person to your group.
Group Evangelism	Have each person in the group pick the name of someone who doesn't know Christ in their neighborhood, and begin praying for those people.	Go through a small group study on evangelism.	Invite your friends who don't know Christ to a small group party to share a little about the community you have as a group. You may find that some of your friends want to attend your group.
Local Missions	Spend some time as a group mapping your neighborhood. Who doesn't know Christ? You could also identify those in your spheres of influence whom you could invite to dinner.	As a group, serve together in your local community. You could volunteer at a food bank or serve food around the holidays at a local mission. Go out for dessert afterward and take some time to share about your experience.	Choose to sponsor a need or cause in your local community. It could be a school, a mission, etc. Look for opportunities to serve through the missions ministry at church.
Global Missions	Identify an unreached people group that your small group will commit to pray for. Get more information about these groups from the missions team at church.	As a group, take a class on global missions at your church.	As a group, volunteer for a mission trip focused on the unreached people group you have been praying for.

Churches measure by attendance because it is easy, but is that right? It's much harder to measure a work of grace in someone's life or discern whether a man is a better husband this week than he was last week. These types of measurements are what we call the *soft measurements* of discipleship, but they are the most important.

Rick taught me this saying: "People don't do what you expect; people do what you inspect." As you develop your small group strategy, you must have a way of *inspecting* whether your people are acting on the vision you have cast. Putting the tool in their hands so they are able to self-inspect makes the assessment and growth plans even more powerful.

ACTION STEPS

1. How are you doing in the area of community?

_____

_____

_____

2. What is your spiritual next step?

_____

_____

_____

3. How are you gifted?

_____

_____

_____

4. Who do you plan to take to heaven with you?

5. What do you need to surrender?

6. Which of the preceding questions was the most difficult to answer?

7. What specific step can your group take today to move in a positive direction toward health?

4

Where Two or Three Gather

Gathering Your Friends

For where two or three come together in my name, there am I with them.

Matthew 18:20

Shared joy is a double joy; shared sorrow is half a sorrow.

Swedish proverb

As a small group ministry leader, one of your goals is to encourage the people in your groups to move forward along the path of spiritual maturity. How can you encourage their growth once they are in a small group?

Understand the Barriers to Joining

As you and your group members invite people into your small group, you need to be prepared for people to give you a variety of reasons why they cannot join a small group. No matter what your denomination or what part of the country (or world) you live in, there are some frequently used excuses people have for not joining a small group.

I Don't Have Anyone to Watch My Kids.

This is by far the top excuse we hear at Saddleback. Following are suggestions we give to our groups:

1. Each family gets its own babysitter.
2. Use the homes of two members who live close to each other. Have your meeting at one home and have childcare at the other home provided by a babysitter or rotating group members.
3. Dedicate one room in the house for childcare and bring a babysitter to the meeting place. Each family can contribute money for childcare costs.
4. Rotate two members out of the small group on a weekly basis to provide childcare in another room of the house. In this way there will be no cost to anyone in the group. But never rotate out a married couple; instead send two women or two men so that relationships are built.
5. Make your group a family group where children are allowed to play in the same room as the meeting. This works best when the children are very small and are not likely to catch much of what is being said. Or children elementary age and older can participate with the group. The positive side to this is that the families learn together. The negative is that you will need to limit talk about adult issues or use of adult humor.
6. High school students from the church could provide childcare as their ministry project. This is an excellent way to team up with the youth ministry and give teens a chance to serve. Check state laws to ensure your church has no legal liability.

7. Trade childcare with another small group. If your group meets on Tuesday and you know of another small group that meets on Thursday, offer to watch their children while they meet and ask them to do the same for your group. This will remove the burden of cost.

We had this problem a couple of years ago in my own small group. When we made out our yearly Group Health Plan, we determined that in the area of fellowship we were using childcare as an excuse. This was especially tough on Lisa and me since with a special needs child we were paying thirty to forty dollars a week just for childcare. But we all agreed that if we believe this group matters, then nothing will stop us. The truth is, it boils down to a priority issue more than it does a childcare issue.

I Don't Want to Share My Personal Life with Strangers.

Many people have a fear of intimacy. They don't want to open up with others and risk the vulnerability that comes with honest and transparent relationships. To combat this, one of the strict rules you must drive home to your group members is that what is said in the group stays in the group (unless, of course, they say they are going to hurt themselves or someone else). People also need to know they will not be forced to share anything they do not want to share. It is important to let prospective group members know all they need to do is show up and get to know the other group members. They are not expected to join a group and immediately reveal all of their personal problems. As they move through the studies and begin forming relationships, the sharing will occur naturally.

One of the strict rules you must drive home to your group members is that what is said in the group stays in the group.

I Am Not Spiritual or Very Religious, So I Wouldn't Fit In.

This is an excuse you hear from many new Christians, seekers who have not yet made a commitment to Christ, and even long-term churchgoers who have been content to just *pew sit* every week. People are afraid they will be forced to pray out loud, answer difficult Bible questions, or be put on the spot about personal issues. It is important to emphasize that your small group is a place where *everyone* is looking for answers and that we can all learn from each other no matter where we are on our spiritual walk. As the leader, you need to communicate this on an ongoing basis.

I Don't Have Enough Time.

This is another frequent excuse. It is true that there are certain seasons of life when we have more free time than others. But the truth is also that we each have 168 hours per week. The question is, how are you going to spend your time? As a leader, your job is to help those in your sphere of influence spend their time wisely. Satan wants to influence our time and keep us busy. God wants us to make biblical choices so that our priorities are influenced by him.

I Don't Know Enough about the Bible.

Many people are under the mistaken notion that they will feel out of place in a small group if they don't have a good grasp on the Bible. They imagine a group of people all reading from their Bible in Greek and discussing deep theological issues. Prospective members need to understand that one of the purposes of small groups is learning about the Bible. No previous Bible knowledge is necessary.

I Tried a Small Group Once and Didn't Like It.

Unfortunately, some people have had a negative prior experience with a small group. Too often someone in their previous group betrayed a confidence, or they just didn't bond with other group members. Remind them that one bad experience does not necessarily lead to another one. Just because I have had a bad experience at a restaurant doesn't mean I don't eat out again. Also give them the opportunity to try out your group by allowing them to just show up for one group meeting or a social time the group is having.

I Don't Want to Get into a Long-Term Commitment.

Whenever you start a new study, give people an opportunity to join for a short duration of the study, usually four weeks. Tell them they are free to leave after that time commitment. Even if they do not stay with the group, the chances are they will eventually join and stay with another group somewhere down the road. You need to let people know up front that they don't have to stay with *your* group. They may not be a good fit, or the time frame may not work for them. Give them permission to go to another group without guilt. In fact, if they express interest in attending another group, help them find one that better suits their needs.

Questions People Have

We have also found that people have a lot of the same questions about joining a small group. Again, if you and your group members know these questions ahead of time, you will be better prepared to handle them.

What Is Required to Join This Group?

People want to know what is expected of them up front. At Saddleback we set the bar very low for joining a small group. You do not have to be a believer or even attend our church. Your church may have a different policy, so be sure to check on that. We just ask them to show up. Once they have decided to join a group, then you can go over the small group guidelines that have been established for small groups in your church (you can see our church's guidelines at www.smallgroups.net/gg).

Will I Fit In Here?

People need to know they can come *as is* and they will still be accepted by group members. The thing I love about my group is that I don't have to shave or change my clothes before our small group time. I can show up unshaven and in my worst clothes and no one cares (with the possible exception of my wife, Lisa). When the group meeting is at our house, our house doesn't have to be clean. They accept us, and we feel that. We are comfortable and we know we fit in.

When you invite people into your group, think of how they will fit with other members of the group. For example, suppose three couples are in a group and the first couple begins to talk about how difficult it is dealing with a newborn and how tired they are from lack of sleep. A second couple in the group says, "Just wait until she's a teenager! If you think you have it hard now . . . you just wait." The third, much older couple says, "Our children were always angels. We never had any problems with them." First of all, the last couple is lying. But most importantly, there is no affinity in that group. Grouping members according to life stage may be preferable. If no one in your group has children at home, then it probably isn't wise to invite a young couple with three kids into your group. It is not always a question of age, however. It is a question of being able to relate to one another. Sometimes groups with mixed ages work very well. If an older couple can give the younger couple tips on how to help that newborn sleep, then you have a bond.

Am I Needed in This Group?

People want to feel they are making a contribution to the group—that they add value to the group meetings. One of the ways to accomplish this is to give them specific roles in the group (more on this in chapter 9). This moves them from feeling that the group is *your* group to feeling that the group is *our* group. As the leader, you may not want to inconvenience them, so you take on all of the group tasks yourself. In reality, your group members each have a contribution they could make to your group. If you are not making use of their gifts and abilities, you not only dishonor them, you dishonor God by not allowing them to be all he meant them to be.

Am I Safe Here?

As stated earlier, group members need to know from the beginning that what is said in group stays in group. This should be reiterated every time a new member joins the group, and it is also wise to remind group members when someone shares something that is particularly sensitive. As the leader, your task is to create an environment in which people can be real and authentic. To do that, you must not only model authenticity yourself but also remind group members that confidentiality is expected and required.

Start with Your Circle of Influence

As you and your group members invite people into your small group, start within your own circle of influence. Very often we overlook the very people God has put into our lives. Your neighbors are your neighbors by design. God didn't place you into the world randomly. He expects you to influence the people with whom you come into contact on a regular basis. That includes friends, family, neighbors, co-workers, people you know through your kids' activities, etc. Ironically, these are often the people we are hesitant to invite to join our small group. Step out of your comfort zone and ask! Encourage

Very often we overlook the very people God has put into our lives.

your group members to do the same. If people refuse your invitation, invite them again later—perhaps when you start a new study that may interest them. People will come because of the content and stay because of the relationships. Even when you cannot always see the results, God is at work in their lives. You may only be one tiny piece of that puzzle, but be sure that you do contribute your piece of the puzzle!

Transition times such as baptisms, weddings, childbirth, and kids leaving for college are great times to invite people into your groups. Some of these times include:

Significant events: baptisms, baby dedications, weddings

Struggles: loss of a loved one, hospitalization, financial trouble, separation, blending a family, single parenthood, health problems

Spiritual steps: at completion of a class, upon becoming a new believer, when a person who has been prayed for by your small group receives an answer to prayer

Seasonal beginnings: beginning of a new year, fall, winter, spring, week after Easter

Starts and stops: new curriculum series, starting a new class, campaigns (for more information on campaigns, see www.smallgroups.net/campaigns, or see my book *Small Groups with Purpose*, chapter 17)

At these times people are facing new opportunities and new experiences. Someone whose last child has just left for college may very well be open to joining a study with others who are dealing with the empty nest syndrome. That same person may have no interest at all in joining a group studying the life of the apostle Paul. When you are trying to invite others into your group, look for studies that have a wide appeal, as opposed to ones that are for more seasoned believers.

When people are going through a struggle, they are also more vulnerable and seeking support. These are great times

When you are trying to invite others into your group, look for studies that have a wide appeal.

to ask someone to join your group, especially if the group is centered on a topic they are dealing with such as marriage, parenting, finances, and so forth.

God uses both pain and change to make people receptive to the gospel and to connecting with others. Look for these key times in the lives of people you know. This is your group's opportunity not only to learn about God's love, but also to *show* God's love to someone in need.

─────────── ACTION STEPS ───────────

1. Who are five people you could invite into your group? List their names below. Beside those names, list the excuse they may use for not joining.

2. Now go back and review the excuse section of this chapter and prepare to counter their excuse with an appropriate answer.

PART 2

What to Do in Your Group

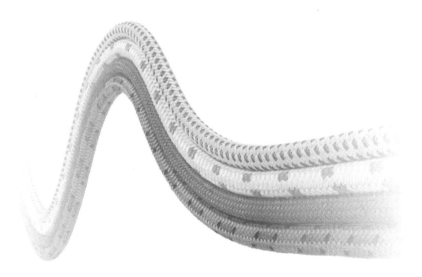

5

Fellowship—It All Starts with Biblical Community

Build a Foundation for Health and Balance

Then you will know the truth, and the truth will set you free.

John 8:32

A half truth is a whole lie.

Yiddish proverb

We have all heard the expression "tip of the iceberg." Icebergs form as the result of an accumulation of snow over hundreds of years. The bulk of the iceberg (about ⅞ of the mass) is below the surface of the water; only ⅛ of the iceberg is visible. Icebergs are white and blue in color: white when the snow is relatively new and blue when it has become very dense from years of compression. Those years of pressure slowly increase the density of the ice from loose and fluffy snow to extremely dense ice. Since it is compressed, the air trapped between the original snowflakes is forced out and the properties of the ice change. It now absorbs all the colors in the spectrum except blue, which it reflects. The oldest, most compressed parts of the iceberg appear to be blue in color.

A danger for small groups is that they may stay right at the tip of the iceberg. Members float comfortably on top of the water and never allow others to see the ⅞ of their life buried below the surface, let alone the dense blue ice compacted from years of pressure. In order to earn the right to go beneath the water's surface, you must provide a safe and focused environment for genuine community to develop so that relationships can go deeper than surface level.

Promote Diving below the Surface

When it comes to connecting with others in authentic and honest ways, your group members will take their cues from you. If you remain on a superficial level, don't expect them to go deeper. As you share your own weaknesses and struggles, you give members permission to do the same and you establish the expectation of authenticity and transparency. If you have had a bad week, don't put on a false façade for the group; let them know about your week. Give them the chance to support and encourage you.

Instead of trying to fix them or give them answers, affirm members who open up about their struggles. Very often, people just want someone to listen. If they ask for advice, give it. But if they don't, just be there to listen to them. When Lisa and I shared with the group the situation with Ethan, it was so overwhelming that we both broke down and cried. The last thing we needed was for someone to fix a situation that wasn't fixable. What did the group do? They just huddled around us and gave us hugs in support. No surefire solutions to fix autism—just caring and being there for us.

Honor the Truth

Many people have no one in their life who loves them enough to tell them the truth. If someone in your group is making a choice that is detrimental to his or her health or faith (dating a married person, drug use, etc.), confront the individual lovingly. Instead of preaching at or looking down on that person, come alongside him or her and offer your support.

In order to speak truth into someone's life, you first need to build trust; otherwise, the person won't listen to you.

How does that happen in your group? In order to speak truth into someone's life, you first need to build trust; otherwise, the person won't listen to you. In order to build the trust, you need to spend time with him or her. Then once you have built that trust, you can speak that truth.

Importance of the After-Group Meeting

My group has our formal meetings on Tuesdays from 7:00 to 9:00 pm. Very often, though, the best meeting happens after that. At 9:00 pm we pray, close, and almost everyone stays for the informal meeting. We start chatting, and before you know it another half hour or hour has passed. Recognize what is happening during these moments. Your members are reluctant to leave because they are enjoying the connections they are making. Topics that did not come up during the official meeting tend to crop up during these moments. "Hey, is your sister feeling any better?" "Did you guys decide what kind of car to buy?" "How do you like the new job?" While they may not have had an opening to ask such questions during the small group meeting, these questions are still important. They are evidence of true community. When I care about you, I not only *want* to know what is going on in your life, I *expect* frequent updates concerning ongoing events and issues that concern you. We call this *the meeting after the meeting.* Although this is not the formal meeting and no curriculum is used, this time is valuable for connection and sometimes is the most important time for the group.

The Other 166 Hours

Outside the formal time when your group meets (for us, two hours every Tuesday) there are another 166 hours a week that you can use to help community form faster and go deeper. This informal group time can include coffees, parties, seminars you attend together, going to your kids' activities, serving as a group, going on a mission trip together, and so on. Think of ways you can use these informal times to help your group grow deeper. The same techniques you would use to build a friendship are also those that will build your group.

First Impressions Create Lasting Impressions

If you are starting a new group or inviting a new person into your existing group, be aware that people's first impression may determine whether they make a second visit to the group. Help new people feel very welcomed. Let them know you are happy they are joining you for the night. Keep it light and informal, but be intentional in making them feel they are entering a safe place, not interrupting a private party. Have group members tell a little bit about themselves, even if your group has been meeting for the last five years and only one person is new. To reduce tension, use a simple icebreaker question such as: What is your favorite television show and what do you like about it? Finding that they have similar tastes in

The same techniques you would use to build a friendship are also those that will build your group.

television shows is a simple but effective way to start connecting members to each other or to a new member. The first impression is usually a lasting one, so you want it to be positive. To make this happen, you can work in three zones:

1. *Before the group meets*—Connect with those who are coming for the first time. Make sure they have directions, ask if there is anything you can do to accommodate any special needs, but most of all, make sure they know you are excited about them coming.
2. *During the group time*—Be sure to greet them using their first name. Be mindful that if you are a hugger, not everyone else is; you have to earn the right to give hugs. Make sure they are included in the group conversation. If they don't participate, ask if there is anything they would like to add. Be yourself so they can be themselves; and smile. And make sure you start and end on time.
3. *After the meeting*—Let them know you appreciate them. Find out if there is anything they would change or add to make it a great experience. Also, ask them to bring a bag of chips or veggies to the next group meeting—there is nothing like a small responsibility to help them feel valued.

Fellowship—the Foundation for All Other Purposes

Not only is true Christian fellowship the glue that will hold your group together when times get tough, but it also is the necessary foundation for all of the other purposes. Unless people feel safe and connected to each other, discipleship will suffer and they will not feel comfortable taking their spiritual next step. They won't reveal their spiritual gifts and abilities, and they won't be willing to join together to serve. If they don't feel connected, valued, and respected, group members will not invite others into their small group (or possibly even to church). Real worship won't happen if fellowship isn't present. But if they do feel connected, valued, and respected, it will be natural for them to want others to experience the same sort of community.

Don't Let the Agenda Drive Out the Holy Spirit

I love baseball. In 2002 the Anaheim Angels were playing in the World Series against the San Francisco Giants. For those of you who are Anaheim Angels fans, you know that this is a rare occurrence. I was so excited, watching every game and loving it! And I was praying—for the Angels to win. I know that it is not the most biblical thing, but after all, this was *the Angels* playing, and that had to count for something!

So it was a Thursday night and the Angels were locked at three games to three games, and this was the seventh game—and our small group meeting was at our house. Since I am a pastor, so of course my priorities are always in focus, I called a couple of guys in the group. "Hey, I was thinking we haven't really had a meaningful fellowship time in a while. So for the purpose of going deeper in fellowship, how about we watch the game Thursday night?" And because I know how guys think, I added, "I'll buy all the food and we'll have dinner here before group." That clinched it. They were on board.

When I went home that night I told Lisa, "Hey, um, a slight change of plans. We aren't going to do group in the usual way. What we're gonna do is we're gonna kinda watch the game."

And she said, "Uh, no. I don't think that's a good idea." Acting as if I was slightly disappointed that we wouldn't be having our regular group meeting, I responded, "Well it's kinda already in motion, and the guys are kinda driving the process." I think I may have shrugged my shoulders in resignation at this point. "So we just gotta roll with it," I added with a small sigh.

The weather in my house was quickly changing—becoming partly cloudy with a cold front rapidly moving in. This became even more obvious Thursday night as all of the couples gathered in our family room. All the other couples were sitting next to each other as Lisa and I sat across the room from each other.

We were watching the game, but I was feeling guilty. So in the seventh inning, when I knew the commercial break would be a little longer, I said, "Hey, let's do this real quick while the commercials are playing. Let's just do a check on our marriages since we're supposed to be doing a study on marriage tonight. Tell us, on a scale of one to ten, how you are doing in your marriage. And at the close, we'll pray."

I really wish this was just a story I made up for this book, but unfortunately it's true. I turned to the first couple and asked, "How are you doing?"

The woman responded, "It's a two."

I'm thinking, *Crap!* But instead I say, "Darn! Well, a two is not that bad. If you have been married for longer than a week, you know that you're going to have nines and tens, and you're going to have ones and twos. It's just part of life." I'm trying to move this thing along; it has already taken longer than I thought it would. I make eye contact with the next couple, but the first woman repeats, "No, it's a two." And then she starts crying.

I'm thinking, *Aw man!* We're coming out of the commercial break and we don't have time to deal with this. I look toward the TV in a panic. Then I make the mistake of looking toward my wife. She is not saying anything, but she is mouthing the words, *Turn the TV off!*

So after thinking about what she said, I muted it. That wasn't quite the move Lisa was expecting. So after getting the eyes of death, I turn the TV off.

I never did see the end of that game (the Angels went on to win that game and the series). Long story short, an hour and fifteen minutes later we prayed with that couple, laid hands on them, and loved on them.

What did the Holy Spirit want to do that night? He wanted to minister to that couple. What did the pastor want to do? I just wanted to see the game. I really, *really* wanted to see that game. But God had another agenda, and the Holy Spirit was at work. No matter what your plan, always be willing to follow the leading of the Holy Spirit.

And buy a DVR.

--------------------- ACTION STEPS ---------------------

1. List the names of everyone in your group. What is the one issue that each of them is concerned about right now? List that issue beside their name.

_____

_____

_____

_____

_____

2. Starting today, commit to pray regularly for each one of those individuals and their area of concern.

3. How can your group begin to get together outside of the formal meeting time? Choose an upcoming activity or event and invite your group members to attend with you.

_____

_____

_____

6

Fellowship — Practical Suggestions

How to Build a Strong Foundation

Dear friends, since God so loved us, we also ought to love one another.

1 John 4:11

Small groups are like quilts, pieced with memories, bound with love.

Anonymous

Genuine fellowship helps us move from just sharing coffee and cookies to being a safe community where we can be transparent with one another. Here are some practical suggestions for your group. They are arranged in a crawl, walk, run order—with the simplest suggestions at the beginning of the list.

Crawl

Meet in a home or some other comfortable setting (such as a restaurant or coffee shop). Meeting outside of the church is much more conducive to creating a relaxed atmosphere. Letting people into your home and going to theirs gives you a glimpse of each other's lives.

Arrange chairs into a circle so everyone faces each other. Such a set-up encourages members to make eye contact with each other, which promotes conversation.

Provide name badges for the first few meetings or when introducing a new person to the group. Remembering each other's names is much easier if they are on display in a simple stick-on name tag. Also, be sure to provide name tags when you add new members to the group. This is often overlooked since the majority of members know each other, but it can really help new members to feel less awkward.

Remove distractions from the room. That includes stacked laundry, loose toys, and roaming pets. If the phone rings, let the answering machine get it.

Meeting outside of the church is much more conducive to creating a relaxed atmosphere.

At the beginning of the meeting, ask everyone to set their cell phones to vibrate. Model this behavior by turning your cell phone to vibrate in front of group members at the start of every meeting.

Provide adequate lighting for reading. While soft lighting may be more conducive to relaxing, your members need to have enough lighting to refer to their small group study guides and Bibles.

Maintain a comfortable temperature in the room where you are meeting. Members who are too cold will be uncomfortable, and members who are too hot can become drowsy. If you have members who tend to be chilly (when no one else is), drape a lightweight blanket or two over the arms of your chairs for those members to use.

Provide icebreakers. Using simple icebreakers can be a way for new people to get to know group members. They can also serve as a fun activity for groups that have been meeting together for years. There are several books on icebreakers from which to choose. A great resource is *What's Your Story? Icebreaker Questions for Small Groups* by Cheryl Shireman (available at www.amazon.com).

Another idea is to write down simple questions, cut them up into strips of paper, and put them into a large mixing bowl. Pass the bowl around and have each member draw a question from the bowl and answer it. Unless your group is very close, be sure to use questions that are easy to answer such as: What is your favorite movie or television show? What game did you like to play as a child? What is your favorite book? This is also a great way for group members to discover they have more in common than they'd realized.

Print a group directory. Every group should have a directory of group members. Pass out a piece of paper and ask them to write down their name, email address, and phone number. Ask for a volunteer to type them up and print them out for all group members (or send it as an email attachment for those who use computers). Such a roster is a must-have in case of an emergency or if a group member wants to contact someone else in the group to ask a favor or something else. Once a year ask the group members to verify that their phone number and email address is current. You also may want to include birthdays and anniversaries.

Celebrate milestones. Take time to celebrate not only birthdays but also anniversaries, the birth of a child or grandchild, potty training, graduations, retirement, etc. This can be as simple as sending a card, as low-key as bringing out a cake at the end of the meeting, or as elaborate as a full-blown party. The important thing is to make group members feel loved and celebrated.

Teach groups to share values, expectations, and commitments up front. Guidelines help avoid unspoken agendas and unmet expectations, which are the source of most of the problems in a small group. We ask our groups to agree on guidelines during the first meeting in order to lay the foundations for a healthy group experience. And we encourage groups to add whatever they feel is missing to the suggested guidelines. This helps prevent problems later on.

Make group attendance a priority. At Saddleback we ask group members to call the host (small group leader) whenever they are going to be late or absent. This encourages accountability and conveys the importance of the small group meeting. Don't let members fail to attend meetings with no explanation at all. It is important to give grace for the many complications of life, but you also need to promote the importance of group attendance.

We ask our groups to agree on guidelines during the first meeting in order to lay the foundations for a healthy group experience.

Rotate your meeting place. Don't have your small group meetings at the same house every week. Very often the leader takes on this responsibility, and it can feel like a burden very quickly. Instead, pull out a calendar and ask, "Who wants to have the meeting at their house next week?" Planning your next month of meetings in advance will prompt other members to volunteer their house as a meeting place. When you meet in various members' homes, you get to know each other on a different level.

Assure everyone that your group is *come-as-you-are* and no one needs to do extra housework or provide elaborate snacks. Then it is important to stick to that. Unless hospitality is your gift and you just love doing so, make your small group meetings very simple and don't go out of your way to impress members with fancy desserts or complicated appetizers. Bottled water and a bag of chips are fine. It is about the relationships, not the snacks.

Use social media sites to stay in touch between meetings. Be sure everyone in the group who uses social media sites such as Facebook or Twitter adds all of the group members. This can be a great way to get messages to each other in between group meetings. You may even want to set up your own group page where you can post messages or photos.

Never cancel meetings due to low attendance. If only two or three people can make it to group this week, go ahead and have the meeting. Don't mistake low attendance for low importance. Every group meeting is important. If only one other person shows up, perhaps that is God's plan. Make use of that time together to connect in meaningful ways.

Build family into your group when children are involved. Have the children call other parents "Uncle" and "Auntie" rather than "Mr." and "Mrs." We do this in our small group. So instead of "Mr. and Mrs. Gladen," we're "Uncle Steve and Auntie Lisa" to the kids in our small group. We know that one day our kids will want to talk to another adult, and we hope that person will be someone in our small group family.

Walk

Start the meeting with some fun icebreaker questions. Be sensitive to the feelings of new people. Anytime a new person joins the group, start the meeting with some fun icebreaker questions. And be sure to go around the room and have everyone introduce themselves again. You could even ask all of the current group members to identify themselves every time they talk that night, for example, "I am Dianne, and I think. . . ." This helps the new person remember everyone's names and feel welcomed and appreciated.

Send get-well cards or visit members who are sick. When a member is ill or in the hospital, make sure you remember them in some way. Instead of doing the usual group meeting, go visit them. Or ask members to make a quick phone call, email, or send a funny card in the mail. If someone is particularly gifted at doing this type of thing, put that person in charge and let them run with it.

101

Have a game night. Instead of the usual study time, surprise the group with a night full of games and fun. Choose interactive games that are simple and fun such as Charades or Pictionary. Pit the women against the men if you have a couples group. It will definitely be a night that you will long remember.

The passing year. As the end of a year approaches, take a few moments at the end or beginning of a meeting and ask group members to spend some time thinking about how they would finish the following sentence: During the last year, my favorite group memory is. . . .

New Year's resolutions. Sometime in January have group members make a commitment to a spiritual resolution. The New Year is a great time for everyone to take the Spiritual Health Assessment (available at www.smallgroups.net/store) and determine what each individual would like to accomplish during the next year to strengthen his or her spiritual walk—perhaps spend more time reading the Bible, make group attendance a priority, read one classic Christian book per month, and so forth. Have members be specific and then follow up with each other during the year to check their progress on those spiritual goals. Then also determine what you would like to accomplish together as a group.

Sometime in January have group members make a commitment to a spiritual resolution.

Dinner for two. Instead of your regular meeting, on meeting night have same-sex group members pair up for dinner. Be sure to go to different restaurants or you will end up sitting with each other. At your next meeting, ask group members to tell where they went and what they ate and to share their favorite story of the night. This is a great way to deepen relationships between members and add a little spontaneity in the group.

Make a surprise visit to another group. Find out where and when some of the other small groups from your church are meeting and then surprise one of them with a quick visit. Bring cookies or snacks, offer to pray for their group, and then be on your way. This is a fun way to show love and appreciation to another small group.

Institute the hot seat of appreciation. Is someone in your group having a hard time? A great way to pick them up is to put them in the *hot seat of appreciation.* Have that individual sit on a chair in the center of the room and ask each group member to take a few moments to express appreciation for the person. It can be as simple as asking everyone to finish a sentence such as, "What I like best about you is . . . ," or, "You are important to our group because. . . ." Or you can give everyone a few minutes to speak freely from their heart to honor this person. After the last person has spoken, give the honoree a standing ovation.

Recognize God's work in your life. Ask group members how God has worked in their life during the past week. This is a great way for them to recognize and praise God. It is also a wonderful way for seekers to see tangible effects of the Christian faith.

Tell a story. Ask group members to come to the next meeting prepared to tell a story. This can be a story about how they were saved, how they were engaged, their wedding day, the birth of their first child, or how they felt the first time they held their grandchild. Throw out some suggestions, but let group members decide on what story to tell. Serve dessert that night and play some music in the background to make the night even more special.

Pick up the phone. When people are absent from the group, call to check on them. Ask if there is any way you can help them and how you can pray for them. Be sure to let them know they were missed in group and encourage them to attend the following week.

Little-known details. Ask group members to each think of three things that most people do not know about them. Tell them to print them out on a plain piece of paper and bring them to the next group meeting. At that meeting, have everyone put their pieces of paper in a pile in the middle of the room. Going around the room, one at a time ask each person to pull one of the pieces of paper out of the pile and read it aloud. Have the rest of the group members vote on who they think the facts are about.

Send a card to a newbie. Whenever someone new attends your group, send a simple card to that person the day after the meeting. Let the individual know you enjoyed having him or her there and encourage the person to come back the following week.

Meet outside of group time for social events. Have meals together, go to a movie, go to a ball game, or do something you all enjoy. Spending time together outside your regular group meetings is a great way to bond with group members and create lasting memories.

Spending time together outside your regular group meetings is a great way to bond with group members and create lasting memories.

Create a safe environment for group members. We want people to be heard and feel loved. It's not the group's job to fix them. A spiritually healthy group understands this.

Keep sharing confidential. It's important to keep anything that is shared within the group strictly confidential. That becomes difficult once you start doing emails and prayer requests. You have to be careful what you share.

Follow biblical principles for conflict resolution. It's important to immediately resolve any conflicts or concerns by following the principles of Matthew 18:15–17, which begins with going directly to the person with whom you have an issue. When somebody in a small group comes to the host and says, "I've got a problem with so and so," the host's first response should be, "Have you discussed it with him [or her]?" If the person hasn't, the host needs to say, "I don't want to hear about it until you have had an opportunity to share it with him [or her]." Matthew says if your brother has sinned against you, you must go and talk to him. If he hears you, you have made a brother. As a leader, that will help you immediately. If I have a problem with Jeff and I go to Mark to complain about him, I am just gossiping. I am not doing anything but trying to get Mark on my side so we can go beat up Jeff. Don't let that happen in your small groups.

Do a study with another small group. Get together with another group from your church and do a small group study together. Find out which other groups meet on the same night as yours and invite them to join you. This is a great way to not only expand the horizons of your small group but also get to know other members of your church.

Share your life line. Give all the group members a piece of graph paper. Ask them to think about the high points and low points of their lives and draw a line across the graph paper to display those points. After everyone has finished their life line, go around the room and ask members to share a little about those high and low points and how God helped them get through each stage. If there are people in your group who are relatively new Christians, ask them to include the point when they accepted Christ into their life. This exercise works better with groups that have been together for a while and have built up a level of trust.

Family photo night. Ask group members to bring in a photo of their family. This can be one photo of the entire group or individual photos of each family member. Then ask everyone to share the photos, giving names and perhaps a word to describe each person depicted in the photo (sweet, fun, stubborn, devoted, etc.). Be sure to include the option of bringing in pet pictures for the pet lovers in your group.

Personal photo night. Ask group members to bring in their favorite photo of themselves. If you have an all-couples group, you may want to ask members to bring in their wedding photos and share one fun fact about their wedding day. Tell group members to be creative and have fun with this. The photo does not have to be recent; it can be a baby photo or a snapshot of a favorite Halloween costume.

Baby face. Ask members to bring in one of their baby photos. Have a box to collect the photos as they enter the room. Once everyone has arrived, spread all the photos out on a table and then spend a few minutes trying to match the adult with the baby.

Run

Go to baptisms together. Whenever your church has baptisms, celebrate those victories by attending as a group. This is especially important if someone in your group is being baptized. Pool your money and buy a gift for the person being baptized, wrap it in beautiful paper, and include a card with everyone's signature.

Going through a spiritual retreat together will bond your group in ways that would be impossible to replicate in a weekly small group meeting.

Plan an overnighter. Arrange for an adults-only weekend or a family getaway. Do something fun such as going to an amusement park or visiting a nearby state or national park. Take lots of digital photos and send copies via email to all of the group members when you return.

Spiritual retreat. Plan a weeklong or overnight spiritual retreat for the adults. Going through such an experience together will bond your group in ways that would be impossible to replicate in a weekly small group meeting. Choose a place that is isolated so you will be able to unplug and enjoy the solitude. Encourage group members to seek guidance from God and perhaps even journal through the experience.

Vacation together. Plan a family-oriented vacation and take all of the kids along. This gives your kids a chance to be part of the small group, and it allows members to get to know each other's children. If you have a singles group or an empty nest group, plan for a vacation experience without kids such as white-water rafting, hiking, visiting a national park, going on a cruise, or some other adult-oriented activity.

Group Evaluation Card

A very simple way to improve your group and increase members' sense of ownership is to ask them to fill out a group evaluation card (go to www.smallgroups.net/resources and download "Small Group Evaluation"). At Saddleback we use a simple card that asks very basic questions such as: What do you like about the group? What do you like least? What's one thing you would add to the group? What's one thing you would drop or deemphasize? We also leave a blank spot for other comments and make it optional to include their name.

———————— ACTION STEPS ————————

1. What steps from this chapter can you implement in your group?

2. Who can help you implement these steps?

3. When will you do it?

7

Discipleship—Encouraging Spiritual Growth in Your Members

Developing Your Members

I long to see you so that I may impart to you some spiritual gift to make you strong—that is, that you and I may be mutually encouraged by each other's faith.

Romans 1:11–12

Men do not decide their future. They decide their habits and their habits decide their future.

Anonymous

What has made the greatest impact on your spiritual growth? If you're like me, the answer isn't a sermon, a lesson, or even a book; the answer is a person who was willing to invest time in you. Ron Swiger was one of the first guys who intentionally poured into my life. As I mentioned in the introduction, he put me through leadership development training without my knowing it. He never asked me if I wanted to do something, he just brought me along. He never said he was teaching me this or that but instead modeled ministry. No matter what the situation, I received a life lesson through it. Looking back I can see how Ron's example shaped the way I do ministry almost a decade later.

Who has made a significant impact on *your* spiritual growth? Specifically, what did that person do that stimulated growth in your life? What could you do to have that kind of impact on someone else's life? What could you do to have that kind of impact on the members of your small group?

Discipleship in Small Groups

One of my favorite verses about discipleship is found in Mark 3:14. It says that Jesus "appointed twelve . . . that they might be with him and that he might send them out to preach."

The first part of the disciples' training was just being in relationship with Christ. Before he sent them out to preach, he first invited them to just *be with him*—walk with him, eat with him, and watch how he handled conflicts. Discipleship—growing to be more like Christ—is developed in relationships with people.

Help Group Members Understand Their Role

Every person in your group is an important part of the process—not just the leader. The sooner your group members realize this, the healthier your group will be, and the easier your job will become. Ideally, as time goes by and relationships become stronger and deeper, group members will earn the right to speak into each other's lives and help each other live the truths found in the Bible. Everyone plays a role in each other's lives, whether you realize it or not.

Impress from a Distance; Impact Up Close and Personal

Our traditional idea of a leader is someone who is slightly above those he or she leads, someone who keeps a slight distance from the followers. A Christian leader, however, should follow the example of Christ, who came to serve. "For even the Son of Man did not come to be served, but to serve, and to give his life as a ransom for many" (Mark 10:45). God entrusted to you that group of people you meet with every week. As a leader, your role is to serve them by determining where they are in their spiritual journey and encouraging them to take their next spiritual step. While small group studies are an important part of your small group meetings, do not make the mistake of thinking those studies are the *reason* for meeting. Your focus should be on developing people, not discussing a passage.

Ideally, as time goes by and relationships become stronger and deeper, group members will earn the right to speak into each other's lives and help each other live the truths found in the Bible.

The Goal Is Transformation, Not Information

The goal is *not* to get through the study every week, although good small group studies are wonderful tools for generating discussion and learning Scripture. While you may get through the study, the goal is *not* to finish the curriculum. The goal is to get the Word of God and the truth of God into the lives of the people who sit in that room with you. You want to see it become more than just another learning experience. You want to see the truth of the Scripture reflected in the lives of group members.

Spiritual Growth Is More Caught than Taught

Is your life a reflection of your faith? If it were possible for your group members to live your spiritual life for 24 hours, at the end of that 24 hours would they want to give it back to you, or would they want to hang on to it? Is your relationship with your spouse, children, friends, and co-workers a reflection of your Christian faith? Do you walk the walk or just talk the talk? These are the true requirements of leadership—not that you have it all together, but that each day you are making choices that honor God and that you are always trying to move in the right direction.

The goal is to get the Word of God and the truth of God into the lives of the people who sit in that room with you.

How you live your life says much more about your leadership ability than how you lead a group meeting. You cannot teach what you don't know. You may be a biblical scholar, but if you don't lead an honest life and try to have loving relationships, then all of that knowledge is meaningless. "If I give all I possess to the poor and surrender my body to the flames, but have not love, I gain nothing" (1 Cor. 13:3). The best thing you can do for your group members is to be in close relationship with Christ. If you have that, everything you do will flow from that relationship, and you will *show* your group members how to worship God rather than merely *tell* them how.

Discipleship Involves All of the Biblical Purposes

Of the five biblical purposes, discipleship is the most difficult to define because it is holistic in nature and encompasses all of the other purposes. When you are healthy and growing in spiritual maturity:

you have authentic relationships with other Christians (fellowship)

you are learning biblical principles (discipleship)

you are using your gifts and abilities to serve others (ministry) you are reaching out to others (evangelism)

you are praising God and surrendering your life to him (worship)

So the best way to promote spiritual growth in yourself, in others, and in your group is to work on balancing those five biblical purposes in your life and in your group.

Balance Health of Individuals and Health of the Group

As the leader of your group, you always need to be thinking about how to encourage the health not only of every individual in your group but also of the overall group. Individual group members need to balance the biblical purposes in their life, and the group as a whole also needs to balance those purposes.

As mentioned earlier, have everyone in your group take the Spiritual Health Assessment once a year and develop a Spiritual Health Plan with their spiritual next steps for the upcoming year. Unlike physical checkups that are done by medical professionals, each member of your group can check his or her own spiritual vital signs with a quick assessment. Once they have completed the assessment and created a Personal Health Plan (see table 3.2), encourage everyone to pair up with someone else in the group to form a spiritual partnership. These spiritual partners (of the same sex) can share their plans with each other and encourage those next steps throughout the year.

Spiritual Partners

Spiritual partners are there to encourage and support each other. As their relationship develops, they discover the answers to the following questions:

Who are you? This is hearing your partner's story and finding out who he or she really is.

How are you? This is a bit more personal as you begin to discover hopes, challenges, and needs. Not every day is fine or perfect; it is real, with ups and downs.

How can I help you? This is when you have reached the level where you can honestly speak into each other's lives. You must earn the right to fulfill this role. It takes time, trust, and transparency.

Let me give you an example from my group. The guys have breakfast occasionally. During a discussion it seemed quite obvious that one of the guys wasn't attending church on the weekends. We began to explore that, and he said, "You know, it's really not very convenient. It takes me about thirty-five to forty minutes just to drive to church, and on Saturday we have other plans. We do dinner with family or friends." He continued, "Sunday I can't go to the early service because I'd miss the tee time with the guys I play golf with on Sunday mornings. And of course the later services would be in the middle of the game." Then he added, "Sunday nights I'm starting to think about my week and what's going to happen with my business. So I feel like I need to kind of hunker down to get ready for the week."

I said, "Come on. We have six services. This is not an issue of not being able to get there; this is an issue of priority. You've not made church attendance a priority yet, and you need to give up something in your life in order to make room for attending church."

How could I talk that honestly with him? First, because I have a relationship with him, and I know what's going on in his life. Second, he knows I love him. We need to have people in our lives who love us enough to tell us what we need to know.

Maintain a Spiritually Healthy Diet

If you asked your kids each night what they would like to have for dinner, chances are your family would exist on a steady diet of pizza, ice cream, and cake. If you always ask your group members what type of study they would like to do next, you may end up with a diet that is just as imbalanced as the meals your kids choose. Instead, through using the Spiritual Health Assessment, you can average your members' scores and determine where, as a group, you are the weakest. If evangelism is a weakness, then you need to do a small group study on evangelism during the next six months. Just like a healthy diet for your family, a spiritually healthy diet for your small group will be balanced.

Keep It Interesting

Keep in mind that your group is composed of many people with many different likes and interests. Some will love doing in-depth studies, others will prefer getting together for social occasions, and others would rather do community projects as a group. Be sure to include all types of opportunities for growth, not just those that appeal to you. Brainstorm with the group and ask for their suggestions. Empower them to think of the group as *our* group. Not only does this keep things more interesting for everybody, but it also gives everyone a sense of ownership. By using your group planner, you can set out some goals for the next six months.

We need to have people in our lives who love us enough to tell us what we need to know.

One of the significant ways to keep their interest is to vary the curriculum. At Saddleback we say that people sign up for a small group for content (to do a particular study) but they stay for the relationships. By varying the type of content, you can add to the overall experience for your group members. For example, if you have never used a video-based small group study, you may want to try one. They typically come with a study guide for each group member and a teaching DVD to be viewed at the beginning of each session. We have discovered there are tremendous advantages to video curriculum. They take the pressure off the leader and provide sound biblical teaching on a consistent basis. They also usually provide good discussion questions. Video curriculum is a good way to take your members deeper into the Word and deeper into each other's lives through a relaxed and comfortable format—your television.

The Power of Encouragement

As the leader of your small group, sometimes the most important thing for you to accomplish is simply encouraging your members. You need to continually look for ways to speak words of affirmation and encouragement into the lives of each member.

I love Hebrews 3:13: "But encourage one another daily, as long as it is called Today, so that none of you may be hardened by sin's deceitfulness." You know what that passage tells me? Encouragement is a powerful tool that has the power to restrain sin. Use it!

A Look, a Word, and a Touch

Pastor Rick taught me that your small group members need your encouragement through "a look, a word, and a touch." Give them your full attention and make eye contact with them when they speak. Speak simple words of encouragement that will breathe into their soul. Provide a simple touch such as a handshake, a hand on the shoulder, or a hug.

It's important to believe in them because if you do, they're going to grow. If they feel loved and affirmed, they will be willing to take more risks. As you model this type of behavior, it will soon become normal in the group, and you will find encouragement growing between members.

Constantly Encourage Spiritual Next Steps

Just as our Spiritual Health Assessment is broken into crawl, walk, and run steps, you and your group members need to think of ways to encourage each other in a crawl, walk, run manner. For example, during a group discussion, Jim mentions that he would like to reconcile with his estranged father. Instead of suggesting he drive to his father's house for a visit this weekend, think of small steps that could lead to that result. For instance:

Crawl—Send a "thinking of you" card to his father.
Walk—Give his father a call on the phone.
Run—Go for a visit.

Group members will be more willing to take smaller steps. As they are successful in those smaller steps, they will be more comfortable taking the more difficult steps. So how can you do this with the people in your group? Think through the opportunity and risk as well as the fear and faith.

Opportunity/Risk, Fear/Faith

Whenever your small group members (or you) are presented with an opportunity to grow, a certain degree of risk is always involved. It may be a risk of time or money or of stepping out of a comfort zone. At that moment we have two options: step out in faith or be paralyzed by fear and refuse to move at all (see figure 7.1).

The key to preventing paralysis is lowering the bar of risk and providing your group members with the opportunity to become involved at a *crawl* level. Once they have been successful at the crawl level, which builds their faith, then you can ask for a *walk* commitment when the next opportunity comes along. Unfortunately, in our desire to help people overcome a problem or take an opportunity, we sometimes make

Figure 7.1

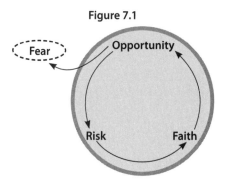

suggestions that are too difficult and ask for a *run* step. Doing so almost ensures they will be paralyzed by fear and brush off your suggestion. The risk level is just too high. If you lower the bar and ask for a crawl commitment, you reduce the risk and increase the likelihood of getting a positive response. This is a pattern of behavior that was true in biblical times and is still true today.

In 1 Samuel 17 we find a wonderful example of the opportunity/risk or fear/faith cycle played out in the life of David. His first opportunity was shepherding sheep. David was quite young, so perhaps he was a little fearful of such responsibility. He accepted the risk, however, and it built his faith. His next opportunity came in the form of a bear. He took the risk, killed the bear, and his faith continued to grow. At some point, David must have realized that whenever he stepped out of his comfort zone in faith, God guided and protected him. The risk level continued to increase when David faced a lion. He took the risk, killed the lion, and fed his faith. Finally, the day came when he squared off face-to-face against Goliath, the mighty giant. Because of his faith, David was able to kill the giant with a handful of stones. But how do you think it might have ended if Goliath had been David's *first* opportunity for risk? Would he have stepped forward in faith, or

If they feel loved and affirmed, they will be willing to take more risks.

would he have turned and run for the hills? He was able to face the seemingly impossible task of slaying Goliath with a handful of rocks because he had already traversed through the crawl, walk, run stages.

Everybody has a threshold of pain or risk they are willing to accept. Their response is going to be determined by the degree of risk and their degree of faith. If a group member's degree of faith does not match the degree of risk, he or she is going to avoid the opportunity for growth. On the other hand, if you lower the risk, you will provide opportunities for the individual's faith to grow. Then at the next opportunity, he or she will not only be more likely to take a risk but also will be able to move up to a new level of risk.

You also have to remember that what does not seem like a big deal to you may be a very big deal to someone else. In the example we used earlier, if you have a close relationship with your father, you may think it is odd to be so nervous about making a visit. But you do not know what happened in the past to cause the estrangement, so be careful to avoid generalizations and assumptions based on your own experiences.

Just Ask Them to Pray about It

A number of years ago I was sitting on our patio when Steve Rutenbar, our missions pastor, leaned over to me and said, "I want to talk with you about our upcoming Africa trip." I said, "I've got it on my calendar, and I'm praying for your trip." He said, "I don't want you to only pray about it. I want you to pray about going on it."

That was not what I felt like doing. I was thinking, *I love missions and I'll pray for you, and I'll even help to pay for your way to go there, but I just don't want to go.* At the time we had a two-month-old, and the last thing I felt like doing was leaving the country. So I did the manly thing and replied, "I'll ask my wife and see what she has to say."

Knowing full well that Lisa would not want me to go and would expect me to stay home and help her care for our newborn daughter, I went back home and told her all about it. I added, "I would be gone for two weeks in a remote location. You wouldn't have any way to get in touch with me. You won't be able to talk to me. You won't be able to email me."

Without hesitation, she said, "I think if God is leading you, then that sounds great. You should go!"

I didn't *want* to go to Africa at that point in my life, and if Steve had not *asked* me I would have never made the trip. But I was teaching a class at Saddleback a few weeks later and an African gentleman came up to me after the class and said, "I will see you in Africa in a few months." To which I responded, "Oh, you're confusing me with Pastor Steve Rutenbar. You'll see him." He looked at me and said, "I don't know that Steve. God told me I'd see you." At that point I knew I was going . . . sigh. As it turned out, the trip was awesome and God did more in my life than he did in the lives of the people I'd gone there to minister to. I have been back three other times, learning something new each time.

Everyone has a spiritual next step. Mine was a trip. Your job is to guide your members into taking those steps and ask them to help you take yours. (Check out www.smallgroups. net/spiritualgrowth for other free tools for growth.)

ACTION STEPS

1. What is your spiritual next step? How can you help each group member to discover their spiritual next step?

---

2. How can you begin taking these steps today?

_____

_____

_____

3. What is the spiritual next step of someone in your group?

_____

_____

_____

4. What can you do today to encourage and support him or her in taking that step?

_____

_____

_____

8

Discipleship—Practical Suggestions

How to Develop Your Members

As Jesus went on from there, he saw a man named Matthew sitting at the tax collector's booth. "Follow me," he told him, and Matthew got up and followed him.

Matthew 9:9–10

Leadership is based on a spiritual quality: the power to inspire, the power to inspire others to follow.

Vince Lombardi

Discipleship involves two aspects of our lives. First, it is living in God's presence. Second, it is how we live on a day-to-day basis: balancing God's purposes in our lives, relating to others, and seeking to become more like Christ. Here are some practical suggestions for your group. They are arranged in crawl, walk, run order—with the simplest suggestions at the beginning of the list.

Crawl

Make sure everyone has a Bible. This may seem like an obvious suggestion, but don't assume that everyone in your group has a Bible. If your church does not provide Bibles, ask group members to donate Bibles for other group members. Make sure everyone in your group has a Bible in a translation they can understand.

Have an authentic walk with God yourself. You need to strive to live out your faith and the purposes of God in your own life. Then you need to let the people in your group get close enough to you to see how you do it. Don't give them a laundry list of your activities, but share what you are doing and how you do it. For example, if it is difficult for you to remember to pray, you may want to share that you always pray whenever you are waiting at a traffic light, or right before bed, or when you wake up in the morning. Give group members practical suggestions that work for you.

> *Spend time alone with God, and let your small group know that you do.*

Model the importance of having a quiet time. Spend time alone with God, and let your small group know that you do. Suggest passages they can study for their own devotional time. Share resources. From time to time, check in with them to see how their quiet times are going.

Give an encouraging word. As stated before, Hebrews 3:13 tells us, "Encourage one another daily, as long as it is called Today, so that none of you may be hardened by sin's deceitfulness." Read this verse to your group, emphasizing the phrase, "encourage one another daily." (Other verses you can use include 1 Thessalonians 5:9–11 and 2 Thessalonians 2:16–17.) Then challenge the people in your group to encourage at least one person every day for the next week. During the next meeting, discuss what happened.

The Lord is my shepherd. Ask for several volunteers to read Psalm 23, filling in their own name every time they come to a personal pronoun. For example, "The Lord is Steve's shepherd. . . ." After the Psalm has been read several times, ask people which verse is the most meaningful to them. Discuss some of the ways that God the Shepherd provides for them.

White noise. Ask group members to meet you at a noisy public location such as a mall food court. Gather together and ask everyone to just sit silently and listen to all of the noise surrounding them. Then ask how many of them were listening to the radio or some other form of music on the way to the meeting. Ask how many of them spent some time before they left for work this morning listening to the radio or the television. Discuss the importance of *being still* so that God can reach us without all the distractions. Challenge group members to drive home in silence, praying and listening for God.

Walk

Ask group members to devote a certain amount of time to studying the Bible each week. This does not need to be the same for everyone. The idea is to get them to commit to something that will work for them, not to try to mirror the habits of other members. Keep the commitments private (or just between spiritual partners) so that members do not feel they are competing with one another. One member may commit to five minutes per day while another commits to half an hour a day, and another commits to ten hours a week. The amount of time is not important. The important thing is to meet them where they are and encourage them to increase their time in the Word.

Ask group members to share their spiritual practices. If you have a hard time studying the Bible on your own (or if someone else in the group does), ask other group members how they study on their own. Open topics of conversation on matters such as spiritual disciplines. Seeing how others grow not only impacts on a practical level, but it also encourages other members to know that you are not perfect either. In addition, someone may have an idea that will assist you in your walk with God.

The important thing is to meet them where they are and encourage them to increase their time in the Word.

Rotate leadership. When you rotate leadership, you empower people to move beyond their comfort zone. Everybody can rotate and lead the group either by doing a sentence of the curriculum (asking members how they responded to a particular question or what they thought of a particular sentence), a section of the curriculum, or by leading an entire study of the curriculum. Place the bar very low and ask members to lead the group for a few minutes at a time. If there are enough questions at the end of your small group study, have each member take a question. This is a great way to get people to move toward leadership. There's a fine line between respecting people's reluctance and nudging them to their next step, and you need to know where that line is for each member. But if you keep the bar low and encourage them in a casual manner, they will meet the challenge.

Promote prayer. Your group needs to learn how to develop the spiritual habit of regular prayer. Colossians 4:2 tells us, "Devote yourselves to prayer." Do a multiweek study on prayer. Be sure to include lots of time for members to talk about their prayer habits and how they can improve upon those habits.

Promote margin and balance. We are often so busy with the schedules of our daily life that we neglect our spirituality and our health. Ask group members how much time they devote to just sitting in silence with the Lord. Challenge them to give up one activity (for example, half an hour of television at night) and instead spend that time in silence with God. Encourage members to sit in a quiet room and, if they so desire, journal their thoughts.

Suggest the group read a classic Christian book together. Have everyone read one chapter per week and come to the group ready to discuss that chapter. If you are reading a long book, you may want to discuss multiple chapters per week.

My favorite verse. At the end of a meeting, ask group members to bring in one of their favorite Bible verses next week. During that meeting, ask them to read the verse and explain why it is one of their favorites.

Take a class together. If your church offers classes, sign up as a group to take a class together. If some members of the group have already taken the class, encourage them to do so again to support those who have not attended the class. A group experience like this is a great way to grow.

Have a balanced plan of study. For example, annually study one book of the Bible or one on spiritual growth, evangelism, fellowship, ministry, worship, or a life stage study (such as marriage, parenting, empty nest, etc.). Variety makes your group more interesting. Also, be sure to ask for input from group members on what type of study they would like to do next.

Get outside. Plan a trip to a local park. Instruct group members to bring along a Bible and a blanket or chair. When everyone arrives, split up for half of the meeting to allow members to go off to a quiet place to sit and read their Bible and reflect. After they have all done so, gather back together and ask them to share any insights or thoughts they had during their time alone with God.

A note of encouragement. Bring a variety of blank note cards and envelopes to your group meeting. Pass them out, one per person, and ask group members to write a note of encouragement to someone outside of the group. This may be someone who is going through a particularly tough time or someone who is taking a step of faith in their spiritual walk. Or it may be a neighbor or friend who does not know Christ. The important thing is for the recipient to know that the group member is thinking of him or her. Encourage group members to either mail the cards or deliver them in person.

Shared Sabbath. Encourage group members to set aside one day as a Sabbath to relax at home and focus on God for the entire day. That will look different for each member. It may be taking a nap or reading the Bible for hours or playing with your kids. The idea is to rest, relax, and focus on God. Spend some extra time that night giving thanks to God for all he has given you.

Ask group members to write a note of encouragement to someone outside of the group.

Share your spiritual journey. Ask group members to share their spiritual journey thus far. Be sure to include details about childhood experiences, important events, and how they came to know Christ. What experiences promoted the periods of most intense growth? What period are they in now—a time of great spiritual growth, a period of slow growth, or a stalemate in their growth? As Christ followers, what can we do to promote our own spiritual growth?

Significant mentor. Ask group members to share who has had the greatest impact on their spiritual walk. What did that person do or say that had such a significant impact? Close the discussion by asking group members how each of them could make a greater impact in the lives of others.

Characteristics of a Christ follower. Pass out pieces of paper and ask each group member to come up with ten characteristics of a Christ follower. After everyone has done so, compile your lists and see if you can agree on the ten most important characteristics. Then spend some time discussing whether your life displays these characteristics.

Take out the garbage. Have a discussion about the *garbage* that is in each of our lives. This may be unhealthy television shows, music, internet sites, books, magazines, and so on.

Ask group members to commit to removing one piece of trash from their life. Have them write those commitments down on a piece of paper and then throw them into a trash can. Encourage members to share their commitment privately with their spiritual partner or another group member for accountability.

Shared quiet time. Ask group members to all read the same passage from the Bible during the next week. Encourage them to read it daily and take notes on thoughts that come to mind. During your next meeting, ask them to share their thoughts and observations. Discuss the wonder of the Bible and how it speaks to each of us in so many different ways.

My song. At the close of a meeting, ask members to find a song during the coming week that describes their spiritual journey. Ask them to bring in a copy of the song to play for the group or the lyrics to read during the next meeting and then explain its significance.

Scripture search. Divide your small group into two teams. Choose a topic such as stewardship or fear and ask the teams to spend ten to fifteen minutes finding as many references to that topic as they can. At the end of the specified time, the team with the most verses wins. Then spend time reading the verses to each other and commenting on how we can apply those truths to our lives. Assign homework to the group members, asking them to come back with ten verses on another topic (honesty, marriage, wealth, etc.). During your next meeting, ask each member to choose one verse and read it aloud to the group.

What's the message? Ask group members to watch television for one night with their family or some friends and write down all the messages, both implicit and explicit, that run counter to the truth of God's Word. At the close of the night, encourage group members to discuss these messages with their family or friends. During your next meeting, ask group members to report back with their results. Then spend some time discussing how we can stay focused on Christ in a society that promotes just the opposite. What biblical truths do these messages contradict? How can we ensure that we avoid being ensnared by this type of thinking and these warped values?

Reading the Word aloud. Choose an evening to read from a book of the Bible together. Select a book and then ask for volunteers to read sections of the book aloud. Encourage members to close their eyes and concentrate on the words as the other person reads. At the close of the meeting, ask members how the experience differed from reading the Bible silently.

Read a book of the Bible together. Encourage everyone to read the same book of the Bible during the next week (perhaps Mark). Ask them to take notes and share the things they learned during your next group meeting. Also be sure to ask them to bring any questions they have. Another group member may have the answer.

Your character. Ask group members, "What character in the Bible do you most relate to?" Then ask them to explain their choices.

Be fruitful. Galatians 5:22–23 tells us, "But the fruit of the Spirit is love, joy, peace, patience, kindness, goodness, faithfulness, gentleness and self-control. Against such things there is no law." Challenge your group members to memorize this passage. During your next meeting, discuss ways that we can be more fruitful as Christians. Bring a basket of fruit for everyone to share during the discussion. Ask members which fruit of the Spirit is most apparent and which is least apparent in their lives. Discuss how they could improve upon those areas of weakness.

New believer. Bring a piece of poster board to your next group meeting and ask group members to make a list of words that describe what the Bible says happens to a person who becomes a Christian. To get the exercise started, you could begin with just a few phrases like forgiven, justified, reconciled, etc. You may even want to invite a new believer to your group that night. Welcome the individual into the family of God and ask about his or her experience in coming to Christ. Not only is listening to a new believer exciting, but it can also serve as a tonic and a reminder of the wonders of the Christian life.

Run

Do a multiweek study on stewardship. During those weeks, challenge group members to make a greater contribution to the church. If they are already tithing, challenge them to give an additional 1 percent of their income. If they are not making any contribution, ask them to start by making a small but consistent contribution every week.

Day of retreat. At the beginning of the year (or the beginning of your small group year), challenge each member to set aside a time (either a few hours or, ideally, an entire day) for prayer and reflection. Encourage group members to think about how God may be leading them. What struggles have they been dealing with, and how can they deal with these struggles in a way that honors God? What prayers has God answered? Encourage members to spend time *being still* and drop all agendas for the day. Allow God's voice to come through, even at a whisper. At the end of the day, ask them to reflect on and write down what they have learned and how they can act upon this knowledge. Ask group members to share this information with the group and choose a spiritual partner to encourage them and keep them accountable.

Participate in a ministry or mission project. Serving your community or your world is a great opportunity for growth. Again, think developmentally. Start serving your church by

> *Not only is listening to a new believer exciting, but it can also serve as a tonic and a reminder of the wonders of the Christian life.*

painting a room. Then serve your community by doing a project such as Habitat for Humanity. Finally, challenge your group to go overseas (or at least out of state) on a mission trip. Serving another culture is very often life changing.

Encourage Scripture memorization and meditation. One way to do spiritual battle is to have the Word of God firmly planted in our minds. We need to know the Scripture so well that we can use it accurately and precisely when facing temptation. Encourage that in your small group by assigning a Bible verse for members to memorize each week. At the beginning of the next meeting, ask them to recite the verse. Initially, use verses that are very short and easy to remember. As time goes by, you can move on to lengthier, more complex verses.

We need to know the Scripture so well that we can use it accurately and precisely when facing temptation.

Celebrate and learn from your life journey. When groups are first formed, most members start out expecting to learn from group studies (and so will you). But the real learning will come from sharing our journey with each other. As we reveal more and more of our struggles and joys with each other, we learn from each other and realize the significance of the group. Occasionally spend a group meeting just catching up and sharing with each other. Stop and pray or give praise when appropriate.

Slow down. Spend a group meeting talking about the challenge of living in our fast-paced world. How does your busyness hinder your ability to listen to God? Together, compile a list of activities that could be omitted from your life (overcommitting, saying yes to every volunteer opportunity, social gatherings that you actually dread, etc.). Then compile a list of better ways you could spend that same time (exercising, reading, pursuing a hobby, etc.). At the end of the meeting, ask each group member to choose one task to omit and replace it with something more enjoyable and relaxing.

Does your life reflect your values? Ask group members to share a story of someone in their life (either living or deceased) they respect. Then ask them to discuss these questions: What values does that person represent? What character traits of theirs do you respect? If you were to die tomorrow, what would people say about you? What do you want people to remember about you, and does your life reflect those values? If not, how can you change your ways starting right now?

Media blackout. Encourage group members to take a break from all forms of media for the next week (television, newspaper, magazines, internet). Instead, spend that time reading the Bible or a classic Christian book. At the end of the week, ask group members to share their experiences. Challenge them to continue the blackout in some manner—such as turning off the television one night per week or turning off the radio in the morning on their way to work.

Fast together as a group. Do a one-day fast together and pray during the times you would normally be eating. During your next group meeting, ask group members to share their experiences. You may even want to consider fasting together for longer periods of time.

Encourage group members to mentor someone else. No matter where we are in our Christian walk, we can always begin mentoring someone else. If you are a seeker and just beginning to explore the possibility of Christianity, you probably have friends who have not even given a thought to exploring Christianity. If you are a new Christian, you could mentor a seeker. If you have been a Christian for many years, you could mentor a new Christian. No matter where you are in your Christian walk, there is always someone just a little behind you (and just a little ahead of you). During a group meeting, discuss those who have served as mentors in the lives of group members. What did they do to mentor? Then ask group members to spend the next few minutes in silence, praying and asking God who they could begin to mentor. Encourage members to contact those people during the following week and ask if they can get together over coffee to start the process. Report back to the group at the next meeting.

—————————— ACTION STEPS ——————————

1. What step from this chapter can you implement in your group?

2. Who can help you implement the step?

3. When will you do it?

9

Ministry—Guiding Members into Opportunities to Serve

Mobilizing Your Members from Sitting to Serving

It was he who gave some to be apostles, some to be prophets, some to be evangelists, and some to be pastors and teachers, to prepare God's people for works of service, so that the body of Christ may be built up until we all reach unity in the faith and in the knowledge of the Son of God and become mature, attaining to the whole measure of the fullness of Christ.

Ephesians 4:11–13

How wonderful it is that nobody need wait a single moment before starting to improve the world.

Anne Frank

When you start asking people what they are gifted to do, their first response is very often, "Nothing," or "I don't know."

Worse yet, all too often the word *ministry* scares them away and they fail to realize God has been preparing them, every step of the way, for a serving opportunity that is specific to them. The truth is that every one of us has a *sweet spot* for ministry. In baseball, the sweet spot is the exact spot where the bat needs to meet the ball to make the most impact. Our ministries should be formed around our individual sweet spots—the place in our life where we can make the most impact.

Helping Members Find Their Sweet Spot

The way we at Saddleback help people find their sweet spot is by helping them discover their God-given S.H.A.P.E. Rick introduced the S.H.A.P.E. idea to Saddleback Church in 1990. The idea was later explained in detail in Eric Rees's book *S.H.A.P.E.: Finding and Fulfilling Your Unique S.H.A.P.E.* The accompanying small group study guide is a wonderful tool for guiding small groups through the discovery process. During a multiweek study, give your group members the opportunity to explore their past, answer questions about their likes and dislikes, and discover what specific experiences they have had that prepare them for ministry.

> *Our ministries should be formed around our individual sweet spots—the place in our life where we can make the most impact.*

Each of the five letters in S.H.A.P.E. represents a specific characteristic in your life.

S—*Spiritual gifts*. What are you gifted to do?

H—*Heart*. What are your passions?

A—*Abilities*. What do you naturally do better than others?

P—*Personality*. How has God wired you to navigate life?

E—*Experiences*. Where have you been and what have you learned?

As your group members answer these questions and look at the path of their lives, they will begin to see how truly unique they are and how they can use their S.H.A.P.E. in ministry. Ephesians 2:10 tells us that God sees us as his masterpiece: "For we are God's masterpiece. He has created us anew in Christ Jesus, so we can do the good things he planned for us long ago" (NLT). Your people not only have something to offer, they have something unique to offer.

"God specifically designs each of us for doing his will on earth. Each one of us is intentionally shaped to fulfill the specific plan he has for each life. Understanding this

Serving (ministry) is not optional.

amazing concept should produce in us a desire to humbly and gratefully accept the role God has created us to fill."[1] The members of your group need to know that if they do not fulfill their role, no one else will; it is specific to them. They have been placed in a particular church and in this group to make a specific contribution. If they do not, the church will suffer as a result.

Serving (ministry) is not optional. "God has given each of you a gift from his great variety of spiritual gifs. Use them well to serve one another" (1 Peter 4:10 NLT). Every member of your group needs to discover, develop, and deploy their God-given assignment. As leader of the group, it is your role to help them do so.

Tyra's Story

I enjoy helping my group members find their sweet spot. A few years ago, after my group did the S.H.A.P.E. small group study, Tyra, one of the members, told me he wanted to get more involved in the area of his sweet spot. I asked him what he had in mind and he said, "Well, you know that I make prosthetics for a living. I would like to do something in that

1. Erik Rees, *S.H.A.P.E.* (Grand Rapids: Zondervan, 2006), 25–26.

area." I was standing there thinking, *How in the world am I going to help him find a way to do this?* I didn't have any quick answers, so I did the only thing I could do at the time: I offered to pray for him. We spent a few minutes in prayer and went our separate ways.

A couple of months later I was in Rwanda with Rick Warren and met a man who told me many of the people in the area were missing limbs due to the genocide of 1994. He asked me to pray for him and his church because they were going to start a ministry to serve these people. I immediately thought of Tyra and asked the man to tell me more about the ministry. He said, "Well, I'm just praying that God sends some people over here who can help train some of our locals as apprentices to make the prosthetics." I excitedly told him about Tyra, saying, "I will commit him to come over right here and now!"

We were both excited and caught up in this moment created by God. He gave me his business card and reminded me, "Don't forget." I assured him, "Oh, I'm not going to forget this one."

The following week in my small group meeting I told Tyra, "Well, God has answered our prayers and found the perfect ministry for you." I told him the whole story, we prayed and thanked God, and I told him I would get the information to him the next day.

The next morning I went to retrieve the business card from my briefcase. I opened my briefcase and looked for the card. No card. I started ripping it apart. This was the same briefcase I had with me in Rwanda. It had to be in there. I got so desperate that I called my daughter into the room and offered her five dollars if she could find the card in the briefcase. I thought that surely I was just overlooking it. It had to be in there somewhere. Maybe she could find it. Of course for five dollars she was more than happy to look. She took everything out of the briefcase and spread it across the room. "No card," she said. "No money," I replied.

But the five dollars was the least of my worries. I was mortified. Our small group knew what I had said, and I still didn't have the card. I went to work on Monday and headed to the office of Bob Bradberry. His nickname is Rwanda Bob because he coordinates all of our trips to Rwanda. As I walked down the hall, I felt sick, literally nauseous.

Tyra was counting on me, the small group leader, to bring him the contact information, and I was already late with the information. Pastor to the rescue! This was my chance to be a hero, and I was feeling like a zero. It's not like I could fly over to Rwanda today, pick up another card, and fly back before our group meeting. Worse yet, I couldn't even remember the name of the man I'd talked with. Without that business card, I had no way to contact him.

This was my chance to be a hero, and I was feeling like a zero.

When I reached Bob's office, his door was shut, indicating that he was meeting with someone. I was so desperate that I walked right in. I told him, "Excuse me, but I'm in a real bind. I need to find a pastor in Rwanda. I can't remember his name."

Bob just stared at me, startled. After what seemed like forever he said, "Can I talk with you after this meeting?" Well, that wasn't what I wanted to hear. I knew it was reasonable, but I wanted an answer now.

"Do you want me to wait outside your door?" I asked.

"No. You can go back to your office. I'll call you."

I mumbled an okay and, a bit embarrassed, exited the office. I started walking down the hall to my office and my cell phone rang. It was Bob. I answered and he said, "Hey, can you come back down here?" I turned back down the hall and hurried to his office. This time I paused and knocked on the shut door. He called for me to come in, and I did so.

He had a smile on his face as he spoke. "That pastor you are looking for?"

I nodded my head. "Yeah?"

"He's right here in that chair." For the first time, I looked at the man Bob had been meeting with.

It was the man I met in Rwanda! He had been sitting there listening when I broke into Bob's office and spilled my guts. He said, "Good to see you again." He had flown over for the AIDS conference we were sponsoring. I stood there thrilled, a little embarrassed, and amazed at the overwhelming grace of God. That afternoon he and Tyra met. On Friday night my small group gave me a hard time, and we all had a few laughs. It was a little tough on my ego, but none of us will ever forget the way God came through for Tyra. The following March, Tyra and his wife, Gina, went with a team to Rwanda to fulfill God's call on his life.

Encourage Shared Ownership

One of the best ways to give your group members a taste of serving is through promoting shared ownership. The small group is not *your* small group, so you shouldn't be doing all of the work. Many small group leaders lead the study, hold group meetings in their home, and provide snacks every week. This is a surefire way to experience burnout and begin dreading your small group meetings. Your group belongs to all of the group members. Sharing ownership of the group helps them move from a *your*-group mentality to an *our*-group mentality—which is healthy for them and even healthier for you.

Don't Lead Alone

When you begin a new small group, initially you will cover all of the purposes. The idea, however, is to look for ways to give more and more of the ministry of the small group away to the small group members. One way to accomplish this is to divide tasks according to the five biblical purposes by identifying *purpose champions*. These are members who are passionate about one of the five purposes who then encourage other group members to fulfill that purpose. So if a group member seems to have a flair for fellowship, ask him or her to become the *fellowship champion*. If a group member is passionate about disciple-ship, ask that person to become the *discipleship champion*. You may not want to use actual titles, depending on how your members react to an official title. Some people would never agree to become the "Fellow-ship Champion," but they would happily take over the tasks related to fellowship. If you sense that sort of reluctance in your people, forget the titles and just ask your members to help out in the area of their interests.

Sharing ownership of the group helps them move from a your-group mentality to an our-group mentality—which is healthy for them and even healthier for you.

Examples of what the champions can do include:

Worship—This person may lead the singing in the group, pick songs for the meeting, or delegate these tasks to others. He or she may also oversee the prayer ministry of the group, lead in Scripture reading, or oversee other similar activities that draw people closer to God.

Fellowship—This person coordinates meals or refresh-ments for group gatherings and may also be responsible for organizing celebrations, parties, and other social activities. He or she helps the group build the founda-tion for community to happen.

Discipleship—This person helps ensure that the group has a balanced spiritual diet and encourages group members to take a periodic Spiritual Health Assessment and de-velop a personal Spiritual Health Plan. He or she may also help the group members partner up for one-on-one accountability relationships as well as help them grow deeper in the spiritual disciplines.

Ministry—This person helps the group find opportunities to serve together within the church in believer-to-believer types of ministries. The ministry champion also coordinates meals and support for group members in crisis (sickness, death in the family, new child, etc.).

Evangelism—This person oversees the outreach plans of the small group and helps the group participate in personal, local, and global missions.

Sharing ownership of the group not only makes the group more interesting for each member but also develops spiritual maturity as group members explore how to best serve one another. Be sure to give members bite-sized roles to begin with. Let the tasks match their spiritual maturity. You may even want to team up members to do tasks together, because taking on a task is always easier if you can rely on another group member.

Don't expect perfection, and be ready with lots of affirmation.

Don't expect perfection, and be ready with lots of affirmation. This may be messy at first as group members experiment and find their way, but it is the path of personal and spiritual development. Be ready to support new ideas. People will need loads of attention after accepting new responsibilities, so be sure to be there to provide it when needed. Two great resources we use at Saddleback are *250 Big Ideas* and *Don't Lead Alone*. (For information on these resources, go to www.smallgroups.net/store.)

Identifying Purpose Champions

There are several ways to identify and select individuals for each purpose in your group:

1. As a group, do the S.H.A.P.E. small group study, which will help you determine the passion and gifts of each member. Then help each person take a step into ministry.

2. Present the idea of sharing ownership to your group members and ask them to pray about who may be best in each role.

3. During the next meeting, ask people to share who they think would be well suited to take ownership for each purpose and why. This creates a sense of being called and chosen as a valued contributor and affirms those who are selected. Once the group has chosen members to serve, ask those members if they will agree to take on the role for the next three months.

It is wise to intentionally rotate roles over time so group members can grow and develop in new and necessary areas of their lives. When they serve in areas outside their comfort zone, they may discover new areas of passion or affirm existing areas. Allow members to team up and think outside the box. Have fun, and remember that the goal is growth and not getting a job done.

Give Away the Ministry

As the small group leader, you need to constantly ask yourself the question: How can I give the ministry away? Even if it's things you like doing and things that you're good at doing, involve other people by giving them the opportunity to participate. Your main goal is people development.

A few years ago, Saddleback started a satellite service in San Clemente, about twenty miles away. We wanted to expand from our Lake Forest location and move toward having multiple sites. To prepare for that, another pastor and I went to Dallas to attend a conference on how to set up multisite services. We met some people from another church that did multisites through satellites. At the time, we thought satellite was the technology we needed to kick off our new regional site. We were told that we needed to connect with a church in Oklahoma City. Eventually we asked the Oklahoma City church to share some information and some of their contacts with us. They agreed and gave us the business card of the owner of the company they had contracted to do their work.

The other pastor and I looked at the business card and then looked at each other. Guess where this business was located? Lake Forest, California! In our city! But wait, it gets better.

Later that night we wondered what the chances were that this guy went to our church. So we entered his name in our database, and he popped up immediately. Not only was he in our database, he was a *member*. But it gets even better. He was in a small group!

You motivate people by asking what they have to offer God's kingdom.

So we flew from Southern California to Dallas to connect with a church in Oklahoma to find out that the person we needed was not only in Lake Forest, not only in our very own church, but in one of our small groups. That is what you call poor stewardship.

You motivate people by asking what they have to offer God's kingdom. It wasn't that this guy didn't want to help out the church. He had been at Saddleback for three years, but no one had asked him. Don't make that mistake. Find out the sweet spot of every one of your small group members. First Corinthians 12:7 tells us that *spiritual gifts were given for the common good of the body*. Encourage your group members to use those gifts to serve the group, the church, the community, and even the world.

Nurture Their Servant Hearts

Christianity is synonymous with serving. Every Christian was meant to serve. Christ is the perfect model of someone with a servant's heart. "So he got up from the table, took off his robe, wrapped a towel around his waist, and poured water into a basin. Then he began to wash the disciples' feet, drying them with the towel he had around him" (John 13:4–5 NLT). The best way to develop servant hearts in your group members is to get them involved in serving and to remind them of *why* they are serving—to show the love of Christ to others. When I think of people with a servant's heart, I often think of a man who attended the previous church where I worked.

One day I was reading an article in a California-based magazine that was about the highest-paid executives in our county. As I read it, I spotted a name and thought, *That's funny, one of these guys has the same name as a man in our church.* Only the guy at the church certainly didn't make millions of dollars a year. He was a thin man with a scruffy beard. Every weekend I saw him cleaning up after others and picking up discarded programs after the service. I also knew him because he was a small group leader. Occasionally I saw him and waved, and he always waved back and gave me a big smile as he went about cleaning up the trash.

Christianity is synonymous with serving.

Well, eventually I learned that the guy who picked up the trash after services was the same guy who had been highlighted in that magazine. Yes, he did make millions of dollars a year. So that weekend I walked up to him and said, "I just want to let you know you're my new best friend." Okay, I didn't really say that, but in my darker moments I might have considered that possibility. Instead, I walked up to him and told him that I had recently read that article. His immediate response was, "I hate that article."

After a brief talk I asked him, "Why do you do what you do? You could hire our whole facilities staff to do what you do and you wouldn't even feel it. Why do you spend your time picking up other people's trash?"

I'll never forget his answer. He walked me up into the balcony, and once we were up there he said, "Do you see this chair?"

I said, "Yep. I see it, along with 200 others up here."

His face softened, and I immediately regretted that dumb comment as he spoke. "That is the chair where I found Christ," he said. "I will never reach any kind of status that will prevent me from serving him in his house."

It was a moving reminder of what it truly means to be a servant. I will never forget it.

Get into the Game

One of the most rewarding things a small group can do is serve together. There is no substitute for working together as a team in the service of others. Service projects create a unique bond among the small group members, and they often provide opportunities for evangelism.

Now that you have two great reasons to serve together as a small group, you will soon discover that service projects are one of the most challenging things to coordinate with your small group. Well-intended small group leaders are often brought to their knees trying to find service projects that work for the busy schedules of the group members.

I recently discovered a useful website that is helpful for small group leaders—WYDopen (www.wydopen.com). What I find unique about WYDopen is that it allows you to filter service projects based on your small group's needs, and you can sign up immediately. Gone are the days where you need to call the event organizer to get the details and try to coordinate the service project with your small group. You can sign up for an event on the site, and it will allow you to send an invitation to your entire small group by entering their email addresses. With a few short clicks, you can empower your small group with a service project that they will never forget and enrich the lives of others through your service.

You can also post your service project at WYDopen for free. This is a great way for you to solicit more help to serve and also plant a seed for evangelism for those surfing the web. Who knows, maybe someone looking online for serving opportunities will find your project and find Christ at the same time!

—————— ACTION STEPS ——————

1. What are you gifted to do?

2. What passions do you have?

3. What do you naturally do better than others?

4. How has God wired you to navigate life?

5. Where do you need to jump in and serve?

10

Ministry—Practical Suggestions

How to Mobilize Your Members

Whoever serves me must follow me; and where I am, my servant also will be. My Father will honor the one who serves me.

John 12:26

Being good is commendable, but only when it is combined with *doing* good is it useful.

Anonymous

In most groups, ministry, evangelism, and worship tend to be growth areas. So here are some practical suggestions for your group for ministry. They are arranged in crawl, walk, run order—with the simplest suggestions at the beginning of the list.

Crawl

Apply the truths you learn. The last thing many believers need today is to go to another Bible study. Growing as a Christian requires more than just knowledge. Continually look for ways your small group members can put into practice the things you are learning each week. Challenge group members to take action steps, and model that behavior yourself by making commitments to action steps yourself. A great website to check out is www.wydopen.com.

Do the S.H.A.P.E. study by Erik Rees. This six-week study is a great way to find out how you are shaped. It helps you identify your spiritual gifts, heart, abilities, passion, and experience. Once your group determines each person's shape, they can then begin brainstorming about possible ways for each individual to serve. (For information on how to order the S.H.A.P.E. multiweek small group curriculum, go to www.saddlebackresources.com and look under Curriculum & Groups.)

Consumer versus contributor. Many people choose a church according to what it can offer them. Have a discussion about the consumer mentality we often find in the church today. Discuss the difference between consumers and contributors. In contrast, discuss people in your church who have a servant's heart. Close by asking members how they can contribute more and consume less.

Ask members how they can contribute more and consume less.

Thank the servants. As a group, take a few moments and list people who serve in your church. If your church is large, you may want to focus on one ministry. If you attend a small church, you may be able to list every staff member and volunteer. After compiling your list, spend a few minutes praying for these servants. Then pass out thank-you cards and ask group members to spend some time writing notes of encouragement to some or all of the people on the list.

Community service. God wants your group to be salt and light in your community. So as a ministry project, select a firehouse or a police station and show up with a note of appreciation and a few boxes of donuts or homemade cookies.

I was created to do this. Ask group members: What hobby or activity prompts you to think, "I was made to do this"? How could you turn that activity or hobby into a way to serve others? Is there an existing ministry in the church where you could use your skills? Is there a new ministry you could start? Spend some time brainstorming to come up with ideas for each member.

Walk

Define servanthood. Spend some time discussing what we can do to be servants in our home, church, place of business, and neighborhood. Brainstorm some practical ways that each person can begin serving immediately. Ask each member to commit to do one act of service each day for the next week and then report back to the group on how it went.

Have the group take a class on discovering your spiritual giftedness. At Saddleback this is C.L.A.S.S. 301, which is part of our Christian Life and Service Seminars. Even if some of your people have taken the class already, taking it as a group is a great way not only to bond, but also to create an atmosphere of accountability. Don't just *take* the class; look for ways to use what you have learned and put that knowledge into action.

Have a discussion about how each member can use his or her gifts to serve the group. All members of your group need to discover, develop, and deploy their God-given assignment.

"Make a careful exploration of who you are and the work you have been given, and then sink yourself into that. Don't be impressed with yourself. Don't compare yourself with others" (Gal. 6:4 Message). As a group, brainstorm ways each of you can use your gifts within the group.

Rally them to meet needs that arise in the group. Sometimes you need to look no further than your own group to find service opportunities. Who is going through a tough time in your group? How could the rest of you serve that person? Who has a practical need that your group could fulfill (yard work, home repairs, meals, etc.)?

Take time to tell stories about service. Once the members of your group are serving (in *any* capacity), take some time to discuss their service. Such stories are encouraging to the rest of the group and also honor the member who is serving.

Spend some time discussing what we can do to be servants in our home, church, place of business, and neighborhood.

Dream big. This great faith-building exercise will give you a clue into people's passions and S.H.A.P.E. for ministry. Simply discuss the following questions: If neither time nor money was an obstacle, what would you attempt for God? What can you do to start moving in that direction of ministry? If neither time nor money was an obstacle, what could your group attempt for God? What can your group do to start moving in that direction?

Shhh . . . it's a secret! Matthew 6:1–4 tells us,

> Be careful not to do your "acts of righteousness" in front of others, to be seen by them. If you do, you will have no reward from your Father in heaven. So when you give to the needy, do not announce it with trumpets, as the hypocrites do in the synagogues and on the streets, to be honored by others. Truly I tell you, they have received their reward in full. But when you give to the needy, do not let your left hand know what your right hand is doing, so that your giving may be in secret. Then your Father, who sees what is done in secret, will reward you. (TNIV)

Read this passage together and ask each person to respond to Jesus's teaching by accepting the challenge to anonymously meet a need in the coming week. Then get together the following week and *don't* talk about it! If you feel the need to discuss something, then discuss how it made you feel to serve someone anonymously. Then come up with a plan to serve someone anonymously as a group during the next week or month.

Serve in your church. Spend a group meeting brainstorming about some of the needs of your church. Is there a room that needs to be painted? Could your church use some landscaping work? After your group has chosen a project, make the necessary contacts to make it happen. Choose a time that works for most of the group members (you may never find a time that works for everyone) and get busy! Afterward, have coffee or dinner before going home. Depending upon the project, this could be a great opportunity to involve your kids in ministry as well. If you have a group for men only or women only, this would also be a great opportunity for the spouses to meet the rest of the group and their spouses.

Pray for another church. Compile a list of churches in your area and then once a month pray for one of those churches. Pray for the members, the new people who have just started attending, the pastors, the ministries, and the work of that church in the community. Have everyone in the group sign an encouraging card to send to the lead pastor of that church letting him know that your group is praying for him and his church. This is a great way to start building bridges to other churches in your area as well as show your love and support for other Christians.

Good neighbors. Spend a group meeting discussing the needs of your neighbors. As a group, decide which need to meet. Perhaps you could spend a Saturday raking leaves, baby-sitting for young parents, or even washing and waxing a car. Whatever it is, be sure to choose something that will not offend that neighbor. It is not a good idea to tell a neighbor, "We noticed that your porch really needs painting. . . ." Instead, look for a need that we all have such as raking leaves.

You may also want to bring along some cookies or brownies as a bonus.

Love the single parents. Support a single parent in your church or community by offering to babysit, run errands, mow the lawn, or wash the car. If you have some good cooks in your group, surprise the family with a home-cooked meal delivered straight to their door. Offer to babysit—an offer that is always appreciated by a single mom or dad! And the Christmas season offers a special time to give love to single parents. For instance, you could take the children of a single parent shopping to buy a gift for Mom or Dad. Supply the funds to buy the gift, treat the child to lunch, and help him or her wrap the present. You may also want to consider treating the parent to a movie pass or restaurant gift certificate to use while you have the kids.

Bless the children. Contact the leader of the children's ministry at your church and ask what your small group members can do to help out. Serve in whatever ways the leader needs. Also, find out some way to thank and honor the volunteers and staff in the children's ministry.

Teacher appreciation. Plan a teacher appreciation celebration at a local elementary school. You can thank all the teachers or focus on the teachers from one specific grade. If a group member has a child in school, honor one of the child's favorite teachers. Bake cookies for the teachers and write notes of appreciation for their commitment and hard work. You may also want to ask if there are any school supplies that your small group could provide for a certain teacher.

> *Support a single parent in your church or community by offering to babysit, run errands, mow the lawn, or wash the car.*

Pastor appreciation. Find a way to show your pastor that you appreciate him. Do a little spy work to find out more about your pastor; possibly ask his personal assistant what his likes and dislikes are. Give him something personal and fun, such as a gift card to his favorite restaurant or passes to a local movie theater. If your pastor is married, give a gift they can both enjoy. Or you may want to get a special gift just for the pastor's wife (such as a box of chocolates, flowers, or a pretty candle). Be sure to include a card or handwritten note from everyone in the group.

Car ministry. Every church has people in need of car repair. Find someone who cannot pay for the repairs and surprise him or her by paying for it. If you divide the amount between all group members, you may be surprised at how little it will cost. Before returning the car, clean it inside and out. You could even fill up the gas tank. If the car belongs to a parent, leave some surprise gifts for the children in the car. Something as simple as a coloring book and crayons makes a great surprise.

Service for a season. Every season comes with its own chores. What older couple, widowed person, or single parent in your church could use some help around the house when the seasons change? That assistance may be cleaning out rain gutters, touching up some paint, doing some weeding, raking the leaves, or putting up and taking down Christmas decorations. Is there an elderly widow who could use some help this winter? Offer to keep her driveway and sidewalks shoveled during the winter season. Show up as a group, bring lots of shovels, and have fun!

Baby love. Your church's nursery can probably use some assistance. Offer to help rock babies, clean toys, wash sheets, or fill whatever other need they may have. This is a great opportunity to get to know some of the young parents in your church.

Fa la la. Go Christmas caroling during the holiday season. Include your kids and think about showing up at places such as nursing homes, fire stations, and police stations. You may even want to drop off cookies as a gift. This is a great activity to do with other small groups as well.

I do. When someone in your church gets married, buy a card and ask everyone in the group to include a sentence or two of their best advice for the newlyweds. Or you may want to include quotes on love and marriage. If you know a couple who has an upcoming special anniversary (such as thirtieth), send them an anniversary card.

Help with the Christmas shopping. As a group, offer to babysit for parents so they can go Christmas shopping. While you have the kids, play games or watch a great children's movie. You may even want to include a restaurant gift certificate for Mom and Dad to enjoy while they are out shopping.

Comfort those in grief. When someone in your church dies, reach out to the grieving family. Take meals, send flowers, or even take care of practical matters such as running errands. Ask everyone in the group to sign a sympathy card assuring those who grieve that you are praying for them.

As a group, offer to babysit for parents so they can go Christmas shopping.

Baby ministry. One of the great ways to provide a ministry *and* reach out to seekers is to ask your small group members if they know of any seekers who are expecting a baby. When that baby arrives, put together a baby kit and present it to the new parents. Be creative and fill a basket with fun items as well as essentials for newborns. Buy a card and ask each person to write one piece of parenting advice on the card. Knock on the door, deliver the basket, and be quick to be on your way. A nice touch would be taking a simple meal for the new parents to enjoy. Be sure to make your visit quick and pleasant. As a group, be sure to pray for the new family during your next small group meeting.

Secret Santa. Every child should have a present under the Christmas tree. What family in your church or neighborhood could use your help in putting some presents under the tree? Ask each group member to buy one age-appropriate gift for the children of the family. Insist that the child's parents sign their own names to the gifts (or Santa's name) and keep your giving a secret. Be discrete in delivering the gifts by going while the kids are in school or after they are sure to be in bed.

Run

Caring for the poor. Jeremiah 22:16 tells us, "'He defended the cause of the poor and needy, and so all went well. Is that not what it means to know me?' declares the Lord." Who are the poor in your community? What is your church doing to help meet their needs? What is your small group doing to help meet their needs? Choose a location that serves the poor, such as a soup kitchen or homeless shelter, and commit to serving there as a group once a month.

Serving those who serve. Chances are that someone in your small group or the greater church knows a family who has a loved one serving in the military. Contact the family and get the service member's address. Then be creative as you put together a care package to send to that military person. Be sure to ask the family what that person's favorite snacks are, and include some of those. Also, don't forget to check with the post office to determine what can and cannot be mailed in a care package to a member of the service. Be sure to add that person and his or her family to your group prayer list.

Love your enemies. It is easy to love those who are lovable or those who are already within our circle of family and friends. As Christians, however, we are called to a higher standard; we are called to love our enemies. Jesus said in Luke 6:27, "To you who are ready for the truth, I say this: Love your enemies. Let them bring out the best in you, not the worst" (Message). While you may have no one whom you identify as an enemy, ask your group members to think of someone who annoys or irritates them and then accept Christ's challenge to serve that person in love this week. Report back the following week. How did it go? How did they feel afterward? Did serving that person change the way they feel about him or her?

Make ministry a regular part of your group meetings. Periodically (perhaps once a month), instead of having your regular group meeting, serve somewhere together as a group.

Spend some time brainstorming as a group to come up with possible serving projects so that everyone will have a sense of ownership in the projects.

Reduce, reuse, recycle. Part of good stewardship is taking care of the planet God has given us as our home (Genesis 1–2). During your next group meeting, spend some time talking about how each member of your group can help lessen his or her impact upon the earth through efforts to reduce the waste they generate, reuse items instead of just discarding them, and recycle materials at your local recycling center. Ask each person to take a practical step such as committing to recycle newspapers, using reusable cloth bags for grocery shopping, or ceasing to buy disposable items such as paper plates. In addition, you may want to spend some time doing some earth-friendly projects together, such as adopting a section of the highway and picking up litter once a month.

> *As Christians we are called to a higher standard; we are called to love our enemies.*

A helping hand. Volunteer to help build homes for the needy and the homeless. Do this in your area on Saturdays, or coordinate vacations and take a week to build a home together. Contact Habitat for Humanity for details on how your group can get involved. Even groups with no building experience can help out by volunteering to paint, landscape, or bring meals to the volunteers working on the homes.

ACTION STEPS

---

1. What step from this chapter can you implement in your group?

2. Who can help you implement that step?

_____

_____

_____

3. When will you do it?

_____

_____

_____

11

Evangelism—Reaching Beyond Your Group

How to Reach Others

But in your hearts set apart Christ as Lord. Always be prepared to give an answer to everyone who asks you to give the reason for the hope that you have. But do this with gentleness and respect.

1 Peter 3:15

It is the duty of every Christian to be Christ to his neighbor.

Martin Luther

If you ask a group of Christians which biblical purpose is the most difficult for them, they will almost all say evangelism. This seems to be true no matter how long you have been a Christian. Even many pastors have trouble reaching out to unbelievers. In fact for most Christians, the longer we are believers the less in touch we are with unbelievers. Since evangelism doesn't come naturally for most of us, we often ignore it completely. We must conquer this fear of evangelism. It should be a priority for us and for our small groups because of the five purposes. Also, it is the only one we can do on earth that we can't do in heaven. If we don't obey God's command on this side of heaven, it will be too late.

Our enemy the devil wants us to think that evangelism is difficult and that we will offend people by telling them about Christ. But the bottom line is this: if your small group is helping the lost become found by praying, sharing their testimonies, and inviting unbelievers to a meal or a social activity, then they are fulfilling the purpose of evangelism. It's really that simple.

The Basics of Evangelism for Small Groups

Availability is the key to evangelism. If your small group members become available, God will use them. If they're willing to love people, doors will open. If they can simply tell their own stories, lives can be changed. And there's nothing more exciting than watching someone come to know Jesus as Lord and Savior.

Open Groups versus Closed Groups

Is your small group open or closed? Most small groups think this question is asking, "Will you welcome new people into your group?" At Saddleback we want everyone to be interested in reaching and connecting with people. But how they connect with people in small groups can happen in different ways. So all of our small groups are open philosophically, but the way each group reaches out to people can be very different. The groups may be:

listed as an open group in our database because they want to add new members

listed as a closed group but willing to add people from personal contacts listed as a closed group due to group dynamics, so adding new people is not appropriate at this time

listed as a closed group, but once there is a natural break in the group dynamics, the group will welcome new people again

For Saddleback, the terms *open* and *closed* are mainly for group connections made through our website. We trust people in the groups to know when to add new people and when dynamics aren't the best. We try to instill three things in groups:

1. Personal evangelism never stops, whether the group is open or closed. We want everyone to be taking people to heaven with them. Once people are saved, they may or may not join your group. They might even join or start another group.
2. It is always easier and safer to not reach out, but during campaigns we will all be risk takers. Campaigns are also a good time to assess whether you should stay with your current group. (For more information on campaigns, see www.smallgroups. net/campaigns, or see my book *Small Groups with Purpose*, chapter 17.)

   We want everyone to be taking people to heaven with them.

3. We know there will always be a tension between fellowship and evangelism. Regardless of whether your group is actively inviting people into the group, every member still needs to be responsible for personal evangelism. Just because there is tension doesn't mean we should be paralyzed by it.

Grow Your Group as Big as You Want

Four to ten members is an ideal group size because anything larger than that makes it difficult for everyone to share. But if you take advantage of subgrouping, your group size is actually limited only by the size of your meeting place. Let's say your group has grown to twenty-four people. All of you can gather in one room of the house to catch up with each other or perhaps watch the video if you are doing a video-based curriculum. Then you can divide into three groups of eight and move into different areas of the house for your discussion time. This ensures that each member has a chance to make a contribution to the group study (see figure 11.1).

Figure 11.1

Group Meeting

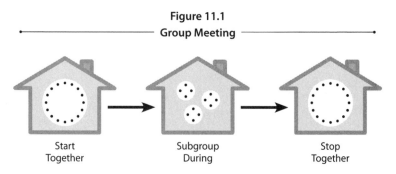

| Start | Subgroup | Stop |
| Together | During | Together |

Of course you will need a leader for each subgroup to facilitate the conversation and keep it moving. Unfortunately, if I ask someone to lead the group, that person is going to give me all the reasons why he or she can't lead. So I don't even ask. Instead I just say, "Hey, could you just take part of the group into the dining room and lead a quick discussion on one sentence? Then we'll all get back together in about fifteen minutes."

After a few months of leading part of the group through discussions on a sentence or two, I take it to the next level and ask him or her to take the subgroup into another room for a large section of the study. Sometime after that I will be able to turn that person loose and let him or her lead the subgroup during the entire small group meeting. Eventually that group may feel compelled to move out on their own. If they do, their leader will already have plenty of practice and the group will have a strong foundation.

Subgrouping in this way will ensure that the doors of your small group remain open to seekers and other lost souls looking for the love of Christ. Not only does it develop leaders, but it also ensures that your small group atmosphere is conducive to adding friends.

When is it time to subgroup? The moment everyone can't share—regardless of the size of the small group!

Men's and Women's Groups

We have found that subgrouping gives us the best opportunity for men's and women's groups to develop. If in your singles, couples, or mixed groups, you subgroup by gender, you can start to get men's and women's groups forming off existing relationships, which will make the accountability circle that much tighter. If I am in a couples group on Friday and a men's group with different men on Tuesday, I can be two different people, which is not healthy. The best men's and women's groups come out of the couples and singles groups. I know this won't happen all the time, but it is something we strive for.

On Closing a Group

There are at least three times when it's good to close your small group:

1. When there has been a rush of new members and the group needs some time to bond and assimilate.
2. When there is conflict in the group that needs to be resolved.
3. When the group has momentarily grown too large for even subgrouping. We had one small group that grew to twenty-six, after which there was no home that could contain it. The members had been subgrouping for a year, which worked out well because these subgroups formed the basis for the five groups that grew out of that original group during the next churchwide campaign.

Pray to the Lord of the Harvest

As a father of two children, a significant part of my God-given responsibility is to make sure they go to heaven. I will do everything humanly possible and use every ounce of my energy to make sure that those two kids know Jesus as their Lord and Savior.

I took it so seriously that from the moment I knew they were coming into this world, I would lay my hands on Lisa's stomach and say, "Lord, if it is your will, I pray that this child will come to know you at a young age and serve you and win many people for the kingdom." And after they were born, every night I went into their bedrooms, and as they slept I placed my hand on their forehead and prayed, "Lord, please touch this child, help her see the need for the living Christ; help her see that she needs you more than anything else in the world. And Lord, I pray that she will not only find you as Lord and Savior but also live strong for you."

One afternoon I had one of those John 21 incidents where Jesus asked Peter three questions in a row (see vv. 15–19). It happened when I was walking around the neighborhood, and the Lord said, "Do you want to see your kids go to heaven?" and of course I replied, "Well, yes, I want to see them go to heaven." And Jesus said, "Yeah, but do you really want to see them in heaven?" and I said, "Yeah, I really want to see them in heaven." And he said again, "Do you really want your children to be in heaven with me?" and I'm going, "Lord, more than anything else." And then the questions turned to my neighbors: "Do you want to see your neighbors in heaven?" I responded, "Well, some yes, some no. . . . Well, actually, all yes." And he said, "Would you pray for your neighbors like you pray for your children?"

Can you imagine if every one of your group members prayed for their neighborhoods like they pray for the salvation of their own family? After that experience I began praying for each one of the families on my cul-de-sac. I pray that each one of them will come to know Christ in a real way as my children have come to know Christ in a real way.

Read how this group took us serious on reaching out:

> We are doing fabulous! My wife and I have just two members and will grow by word of mouth. It's interesting because both are elderly and just love the fact that we began a weekly Bible study. We've done a DVD from Dr. Charles Stanley, as well as two DVDs from Saddleback in "Foundations." We sometimes have to postpone a session due to illness or forgetfulness, but generally we have a weekly session.
>
> The members are amazed at how much discussion we have openly, and everyone is learning more. Our new ninety-five-year-old member is my best friend's mom, and she was very worried and unsure about going to heaven, but now, with the help of one member guiding her back to Bible reading, she is convinced she is going. She is enthusiastic and inspired. We also try to keep our refreshments according to the Daniel Plan.
>
> Best regards, Roger and Joan

Cast Vision

Obviously, it is much easier if you cast vision for evangelism from the very first small group meeting, but it is never too late to start. Sometimes small groups become very inwardly focused, and that's not necessarily bad as long as they are doing personal evangelism. You don't have to invite people to your group, but you do need to build bridges to people.

If you sense your group has become too inward focused, it is time to begin casting vision for the biblical purpose of evangelism. Choose a multiweek small group study on evangelism. While your group is doing the study, prompt the members to think in practical terms. With whom can they begin building a relationship? Which neighbors can they reach out to? How many of their neighbors have they never talked to? How can each group member begin to show the love of Christ in practical ways to his or her neighbors? When I say *neighbors*, it may be physical neighbors next door or people God is placing around you.

To Share Means I Care

Evangelism is actually a way of telling people you care about them. I use CARE as a simple acronym to remind our members of the important points of evangelism.

C—*Capitalize on common ground.* Find something in common with the people God puts in your path. No matter how small, when you find something in common, a bridge is starting to be built for Christ to walk across.

A—*Accept people where they are.* Just remember, you cannot expect non-Christians to like Christians until they accept Christ in their heart. And even then, it is a slow road for Christ to be Lord of all the areas of their life.

R—*Risk sharing your spiritual journey.* At some point in your journey with people you need to share your story. A great place to practice is in your small group. Your story doesn't have to be long, but it does need to be your story of how Christ made an impact on your life.

E—*Expect God to show up.* Your job is to share; it's the Holy Spirit's job to convict. Don't get your roles mixed up. When you share your story, the Holy Spirit will open up doors for you to go through. If he doesn't, then don't break the door down.

Be Sensitive to the Needs of Your Neighborhood

All too often, people think of evangelism as something you do overseas. Unfortunately, some people go on mission trips overseas but never talk to the neighbors God placed right next door. Encourage your group members to learn how to cross the street before crossing the sea.

When Lisa and I moved into our neighborhood, we were very excited to meet the new neighbors. We lived in a cul-de-sac in a neighborhood of fifteen homes. After we moved in, within the first fourteen months, ten homes out of the fifteen were sold. We wondered what in the world was happening. We moved in and the For Sale signs went up everywhere. It was as though they heard a voice say, "A pastor just moved into the cul-de-sac! The party's over! Evacuate!" We started to get paranoid. But what I began to realize was that God was moving a new set of people into our lives.

Unfortunately, some people go on mission trips overseas but never talk to the neighbors God placed right next door.

The first one to move in was a guy named Mike. I walked across the street and introduced myself. I met his wife and his daughter, who was in junior high at the time. It felt like we were off to a good start, until he asked the dreaded question, "What do you do for a living?"

I smiled and stalled for a few seconds. I really didn't want to scare this guy away. We didn't need another For Sale sign in the neighborhood. Finally I said, "I'm in the people business." Then I asked him, "What do you do for a living?" We talked for a few more minutes and then he asked, "What do you do in the people business?" I had to think quickly, and unfortunately I don't do that too well. I went to the dark side of my heart and said, "I'm in life planning," justifying to myself that I help people plan to go to heaven. At that point, I was doing a rather poor job of spin-doctoring my profession.

We talked a bit more and he said, "You know, I'm really not understanding what it is that you do."

At that point I realized I had to come clean. The old *people business* routine just wasn't working on Mike. I sighed and said, "Well, Mike, I'm a little embarrassed, and I didn't want you to think I'm strange—not that you're not thinking that now—but I'm a pastor at Saddleback Church."

Mike smiled and exclaimed, "Saddleback Church! Pastor Rick Warren! I love Saddleback Church! Every Easter we go to your church."

The more I got to know Mike, I learned he didn't quite come to Saddleback every Easter. It may have been closer to every third Easter. He wasn't exactly a regular attendee. But nonetheless, he was the first of my neighbors I began to pray for. How do I, not as a pastor but as a person loving Jesus, get him connected to Jesus? For three years I talked to Mike whenever I had the chance. Then three days before Good Friday, he met me on the driveway and asked if our church services were televised. At the time we were on the internet, but our access was limited to church members. I told him we were not televised, and then I did something that never pleases our technology department. I gave him my log-on ID and password and invited him to watch the service. I also told him I would bring him a couple of bulletins.

Easter afternoon I was in my driveway. Someone in my family (who will remain unnamed) backed up our Suburban before the garage door was fully opened. I was trying to put my garage door back on track when Mike came up to me and said, "Hey, can I get a packet?"

I answered, "Yeah, you can get whatever you want out of my garage. I'm just trying to get my door on the track."

Mike ignored my rudeness and was persistent. "I was just wondering how I can get that packet."

I still had no idea what he was talking about as I continued to struggle to get the garage door back on the track. "Mike, . . . you can start by helping me with the door. And then I'll get you that packet of stuff you want."

He did not come any nearer the garage door. "You don't understand. At the close of the prayer, Pastor Rick said if you prayed the prayer, you should get a packet so your life can go deeper with God."

All of a sudden I said, "That packet!" When someone accepts Christ, we offer them a Fresh Start packet. That was the packet he was talking about! I was so excited that I went to hug him. He pulled back and said, "What are you doing?" Caught up in the moment and a little embarrassed, I answered, "I don't know. But welcome to the family of God!"

To be honest, reaching my neighbors has not always been easy. At times I get discouraged. I am a pastor, and yet at times I feel that I barely can get someone to church, let alone get him or her into a small group. It's in those dark moments that God brings us gifts.

Sometime later, Mike came up to me and told me he had gone back to school. I congratulated him on that decision, and he began telling me about a paper he had to write for a class. "I had to write a paper about virtue, and I want you to know that I picked you. Here's a copy of it." Later that night I read part of the paper to my wife, Lisa (aka destroyer of garage doors).

I never really thought about or classified any individual as virtuous. I do look for strong character in my friends and I shy away from people who use other people, gossip, or purposefully hurt people for pleasure. So I would say that my friends each exhibit virtuous character. Since for this paper I needed to find the most virtuous person I know, I would have to say it's my neighbor Steve.

Mike went on to list my many virtuous traits. As I continued to read about my stunning character traits, Lisa interrupted me and said, "Who is this paper about?"

I told her, "It's me, honey! See? My name is right there!"

Okay, maybe she was not quite as impressed as she should have been. But the point is that even though I could not always see it, God was at work in the lives of my neighbors. God was using me, even with all of my failings and moments of discouragement. And he can use you too, as well as every member of your small group. But it needs to start with a relationship, a simple "hello."

Map Your Neighborhood

One of the things I do at conferences is encourage the attendees to draw a map of their neighborhood and mark each of the houses with a box or even a simple X. While they are doing that, I ask someone to come up to the stage and do the same thing on a large white board. Once they have the neighborhood map drawn out, I ask them to fill in the names of the people who live in those houses and describe where they are on their spiritual journey.

I will never forget the time I did this exercise at an evangelism conference in Poplar Bluff, Missouri. I asked a guy to come up on stage and draw a map of his neighborhood. Then I asked him to fill in the names and identify the spiritual walk of each neighbor. He was clearly embarrassed. He did not know the names of any of his neighbors and knew almost nothing about their spiritual walk.

I sensed his embarrassment and tried to bail him out. "How long have you been there?" I asked.

Quietly, he answered, "About five years."

I replied, "Well, that's okay." Even though it clearly was not okay, I was trying to save face for him. I thanked him and he returned to his seat.

Evangelism is tough for most of us, even the so-called experts. But it is still our sacred duty—a duty that we all share.

After the session, he came up to me and said, "You really embarrassed me."

I said, "Dude, my intent was not to embarrass you. It was just an example, because generally if I polled everybody here, about 85 percent wouldn't know the spiritual temperature of their neighbors, or maybe even their names." I tried to assure him that he was no different from anyone in the crowd.

Then he said, "No. You don't understand. I'm the next speaker after you. I've been traveling and talking so much about evangelism that I haven't taken the time to actually do evangelism." I then thought to myself, *Wow, you should be embarrassed!*

168

Evangelism is tough for most of us, even the so-called experts. But it is still our sacred duty—a duty that we all share. Help your group members to see it as something as simple as having a conversation (without pushing Jesus on them).

Step Out

As your group gains community, bring up opportunities for your group to do a local or global missions trip. Not everyone in your group needs to step on a plane or leave the country. We encourage groups to have a home team and an away team for local and global trips. The home team is made up of those members who stay behind and make it possible for the others to go. The home team plays a critical part in mobilizing the away team as they support them by praying for them, giving financially, taking care of the children of away team members, and so on. The away team is just that—the ones who go away on the missions trip. Both teams are critical, and your group is better when each person is doing his or her part.

——————— ACTION STEPS ———————

1. List the names of five people in your neighborhood or circle of influence, including their spiritual health. If all of them know Christ as Savior, seek out people who don't.

———————————————————————————

———————————————————————————

———————————————————————————

2. What are some specific ways you can build your relationship with those people? Write out what you're going to do and when you're going to do it by.

———————————————————————————

———————————————————————————

———————————————————————————

3. Invite someone from your list out to coffee to get to know them better. Ask one of them to join your group. Or if appropriate (for example, if they are single and you are in a married couples group), tell them about a group in your church that they may be interested in (in this case, a group for singles).

12

Evangelism — Practical Suggestions

How to Reach Out

But he said, "I must preach the good news of the kingdom of God to the other towns also, because that is why I was sent."

Luke 4:43

Great opportunities to help others seldom come, but small ones surround us daily.

Sally Koch

Through the thousands of Spiritual Health Assessments we have done, one of the things we have learned is that both groups and individuals score low on evangelism. Here are some practical suggestions divided into crawl, walk, and run steps.

Crawl

Redefine evangelism as a group approach. Very often we think of evangelism as something an individual does—you invite your friend to come to the church or you share your personal faith with your friends. But in group life, we have the opportunity to think about evangelism in a team sense. Help your group members look at it as a group project. It's not just about each of us reaching a friend or neighbor; it's about the entire group reaching out to all of our friends and neighbors through social activities such as parties. It's about getting the entire group to pray for a collective list of seekers. And it can be even easier for the group to remember to pray for them if the individual members share a few details about the seekers they are praying for because it gives those names on your prayer list an identity.

In group life, we have the opportunity to think about evangelism in a team sense.

Pray about whom you should reach. Pass out paper and pens to everyone in your group. Ask group members to close their eyes and spend a few moments in prayer, asking God for the names of seekers he would like them to reach. Encourage them to write the names down as soon as they are prompted by the Holy Spirit. When finished, ask someone to compile all the names and bring back copies of the list for every group member. Instruct them to bring the lists to your group meeting every week and spend some time praying for the names and providing any updates in progress.

Church lingo. Give one group member a piece of paper and a pen. Ask the entire group to brainstorm and come up with words that are *churchy* and may seem odd to seekers (such as *salvation, fellowship, blood of the Lamb*). After you have made a list, ask members to come up with alternative words that may be more seeker friendly. Have a discussion about how we can all be more sensitive about using words that may confuse a person who does not go to church.

Who invited you? Most people attend church because someone invited them. Most people are also in a small group because someone invited them. Spend a meeting asking group members who invited them into the church or small group. How did that person go about inviting them? How did they feel when they were invited? And finally, ask group members who they are inviting to join them in attending church or small group. If the answer is *no one*, ask group members to commit to inviting someone during the next week and then report back to the group with the results.

Feed the hungry. As a group, commit to bring canned foods to your local shelter once a month. Bring your canned goods to a group meeting and then give all of the cans to one group member who can drop them off at the shelter. You may even want to contact some other small groups and challenge them to do the same. Or perhaps contact your small group pastor and ask him or her to challenge all of the small groups to do this simple act of generosity. Eventually, you may be donating an entire trunkful of canned goods to your local shelter every month.

In a sentence. If someone in your group was asked, "Why are you a Christian?" could he or she answer in a single sentence? Could you? Spend a group meeting talking about the importance of having an answer. Challenge all members to come up with their own sentence and share it with the group. You may even want to do some role-playing and have group members come up with other questions that a seeker may ask, such as: Why do you go to church? Aren't churches just about getting your money? Why do you believe in God?

Invite a neighbor over for dinner. That's it. Have dinner, get to know each other. Don't sell them Jesus or your church; just let them get to know you.

Walk

Break into smaller discussion groups. During your group meeting, perhaps after you have all had a chance to catch up, divide into groups of three or four people. This fulfills three goals:

1. It gives group members (especially the quiet ones) a chance for more prolonged and meaningful conversations.
2. It begins developing potential leaders for future groups.
3. It allows your group to keep adding members while ensuring that individuals talk and are heard during discussion times. You may even end up forming a new small group.

Give group members time to practice sharing their testimony with each other. Commit an entire evening to this or set aside time each week for one person to share a five-minute testimony so group members can practice sharing how Christ has changed their life. It is important to share these stories not only with seekers but also with other Christians to encourage them as they share their stories with others.

Remind and renew the vision regularly. It's very easy for evangelism to be put aside, reducing group life down to Bible study, fellowship, and occasionally prayer. So as a leader, you have to be the one who continually brings the focus back to the value of evangelism. Ask your group, "Who are we reaching?" "Who are we praying for?" "How are you doing at sharing your faith?" "Can you share your faith?" It's very important to review the answers to these questions on a regular basis.

One person. Ask group members to contact one seeker they know and have been praying for and invite him or her to dinner or perhaps just have coffee together. The idea is to move beyond praying for them and begin to intentionally build the relationship. If the person lives too far away to meet in person, consider a long phone call or, even better, use Skype (a free internet service that allows you to use your computer to make calls with video). Ask group members to share the results at the next meeting.

Fill a need. Sometimes actions speak louder than words. Challenge group members to think about the seekers they know and then identify and fulfill a need for those people. Perhaps someone could use some help every now and then with childcare, or shoveling the snow from the driveway, or raking the leaves. The idea is to serve that person and show the love of Jesus in a practical manner.

Top Ten list. Encourage members to always have a Top Ten list of seekers they are praying for. As those seekers make commitments to Christ, be sure to add new people to the list. Challenge group members to take a few moments each day and pray for the people on their Top Ten list. Suggest times that will be conducive to forming this habit, such as upon waking in the morning, before going to bed, or right before dinner.

Prayer walks around the neighborhood. Literally take the next step and as you walk around your neighborhood, pray for your neighbors as you pass their homes. If you see someone outside, be sure to wave or stop for a few minutes and chat.

Offer prayer. Ask group members to commit to asking neighbors for prayer requests. It is not difficult to simply ask, "Is there anything I can pray about for you?" at the end of a conversation. People rarely refuse prayer. At the least, this shows your neighbors that you genuinely care about them. Follow up with the neighbors so they know you are actually praying and not just paying lip service.

Run

Create a new group. If your group has been subgrouping for quite a while, it may be time to release group members and create a new group. If evangelism is a high priority in your group, this can be a wonderful way for your original group to become two groups that can include seekers.

Touchdown. Football can be a great excuse to get together with other men in your neighborhood. The men of your small group can meet together regularly to enjoy the games and invite neighbors who do not attend church. This can build relationships so that after the season is over, they can invite those neighbors to continue with a small group study for men.

On the road again. For many of us, travel is part of our jobs. Many of us also travel for vacations. With a little planning, you can use your road trip as a ministry opportunity. Challenge traveling members of your group to brainstorm on ways they can reach out to others while they travel, asking God to open their eyes for opportunities to show his love along the way. One simple act is to pack a copy of *The Purpose Driven Life* or another classic Christian book. Remember, this must be a book that would be easy for seekers to understand. Then as you go about your business activities or vacation fun, ask God to show you who you should give the book to as a gift. Encourage group members to share their stories with the small group upon returning from their trip.

Plan social events that include seekers. You may remember the story in Luke when Matthew came to Christ. One of the very first things Matthew did was host a gathering with some of his tax collector friends, Jesus, and some of Jesus's disciples. What he didn't do was invite them to the synagogue to hear Jesus teach. He had a party at his house. Follow his example and host a neighborhood picnic or barbecue. Plan to go to a lake or park and have everybody in your group invite a friend. Or have a Super Bowl party. Relax and have fun. The sole purpose of this social event is for your small group to get together with seekers and build relationships. But don't expect lost people to act like anything but lost people. That's one of the huge mistakes we make. We start with this sort of judgment and condemnation rather than just saying, "Man, we're so glad you're here. Come on in." Just remember that they need Jesus. This is your chance to show them the love of Christ. Just accept them.

Be strategic in choosing your small group studies. Choosing a particular small group curriculum can also have an impact on whether your neighbors will feel comfortable attending your small group. Let's face it, a study on fasting or judgment may not appeal to those who don't have any faith. But a study on a particular topic such as the purpose of life may catch a neighbor's interest. A couple of small group studies that have been great successes in reaching out to the community are 40 Days of Purpose and 40 Days of Community.

Bring a friend to Jesus. During your next group meeting, read the story in Mark 2:1–5 about the men who lowered their friend through the roof in order to get him to Jesus. Discuss the significance of this act of friendship, and ask each group member to identify a seeker friend he or she could bring to Jesus. Challenge your group members to be as committed as those men who cut a hole through a roof to drop their friend into the arms of Jesus.

Plan a mission trip together. A great way for your group to reach out to others is through a group mission trip. This can be a trip in our country or an international trip. The idea is to show the love of Christ in a practical manner.

Learn a new language. If you are going on a mission trip to another country, for the months leading up to the trip, attend classes or get together to study the language. You may not be experts by the time you leave on your trip, but the experience will be a great time of bonding and will give you the opportunity to learn some key words and phrases for reaching nationals.

Have a group garage sale. To raise money for your group mission trip or another good cause in the community, have a group garage sale. Be sure to advertise your sale as a multi-family sale to raise interest. Hold it in a large neighborhood and have plenty of group members on hand to greet the customers. You may want to post a simple sign in the garage stating where your proceeds are going. For instance, "Proceeds go to Habitat for Humanity in our area," or "Proceeds go to our group trip to build a school in Mexico." This is a great way to meet new people and give them a glimpse of your heart.

Use a hobby or sport to reach seekers. What are the interests of your group members? What do they like to do in their spare time? These activities can be used to reach seekers. Start a basketball league, begin a scrapbooking club, form a book club, play baseball together on Saturday mornings. Challenge group members to think of ways to be more intentional in their leisure activities. This is a fun way to meet new people and build relationships with those who do not know Christ.

Neighborhood Easter egg hunt. Invite friends and neighbors to an Easter egg hunt at a group member's home. Serve light snacks and hide plenty of eggs for the kids. You may want to have a special area with eggs that are highly visible for the toddlers in the group. This is a great way to get to know your neighbors and provide a fun activity for the kids.

Sponsor a child. Your group can show the love of Christ to a child in an impoverished area of our country or far away in a developing country. Your monthly support will provide the child with food, clothing, and education. As a group, take time to pray for and write letters to the child as well. Send age-appropriate toys or clothing. If your child lives in another country, you may want to include gifts or toys that are uniquely American.

Have family reunions. If your group has multiplied into one or more groups, at least once a year have a *family* reunion.

This can be a social activity or a great opportunity to serve together once again as a group.

Memory book—scrapbook. Chances are that someone in your group loves scrapbooking. And chances are that someone in your group loves photography. Put them both to work and designate them as the official memory keepers. Ask them to take lots of photos of group activities and social events and gather them together in an attractive scrapbook. Then group members can take turns keeping the scrapbook in their home. Some will want to display it on a living room table or kitchen counter where it will get plenty of notice. This is a great way to show seekers who visit your home that Christians have fun.

> *Your group can show the love of Christ to a child in an impoverished area of our country or far away in a developing country.*

Invite unbelievers to special Christmas or Easter events at your church. Unbelievers are more receptive to an invitation at Christmas and Easter than any other time of the year. Challenge each member to extend at least one invitation during those holidays.

Instead of your regular Thanksgiving meal with family, celebrate Thanksgiving by inviting strangers into your home. Contact your homeless shelter, ask a college for the names of some international students who can't go home for Thanksgiving, or just invite some single people who do not have family nearby. Use this season to open your home and heart to others. Not only will it be a blessing to them, but it also will serve as a great model for your children.

Every family has their own Christmas traditions. This year, ask group members to commit to a new family tradition. Perhaps all of you, with your families, could serve Christmas dinner at the local homeless shelter or soup kitchen. Or perhaps you could all make a visit to a local nursing home. This is a great way to not only serve your community but also bring the families of your small group together.

ACTION STEPS

1. What step from this chapter can you implement in your group?

2. Who can help you implement the step?

3. When will you do it?

13

Worship—Experiencing
the Presence of God

How to Experience God Moments in Your Group

Since we are receiving a Kingdom that is unshakable, let us
be thankful and please God by worshiping him with holy
fear and awe.

Hebrews 12:28 NLT

God whispers in our joys and shouts in our pain.

C. S. Lewis

Many people think of worship as the music that is played
during the weekly church service. The truth is, music is only
a very small part of worship. Worship is anything that brings
pleasure to God. In a small group, worship is like a diamond;
it has many facets, and each one adds to the beauty of the
diamond.

Worship in small groups can be both expressive and reflective. It does not have to involve music, but it needs to be more than just something to do. It needs to help your group members pause in their busy lifestyle to be still and experience God.

Expressive Ways to Worship

Expressive worship is done verbally through song, prayer, or words.

Prayer

In a small group, worship is like a diamond; it has many facets, and each one adds to the beauty of the diamond.

Whether as a group or as individuals, make audible prayer a part of your small group meeting. That doesn't mean forcing every member of the group to pray out loud, but give every member the chance to do so. Make prayer easy at first because many people feel very awkward about praying aloud. I will discuss ways to deal with this later in the chapter. Also, make sure you actually pray. I know this sounds weird, but many groups spend too much time talking about prayer requests and too little time actually praying. A good rule of thumb is to limit each prayer request to about two minutes.

Thanksgiving

Go around the group and ask members to say one sentence of thanks to God for something specific in their life. This does two things: (1) It helps the members hear positive things that are happening. (2) It helps them realize that no matter how hard their day has been, there are always things to thank God for.

Music

This can be low-volume music played in the background during prayer time or an all-out worship fest in your living room. The idea is to do whatever works for your group. There are plenty of DVD worship sets for a group to watch and reflect on.

Sharing Struggles

Have group members share with the entire group the struggles they are facing. As they do, be sure to stop and pray for each person. It is important to make the group aware that it is more important to listen and pray than to make suggestions and try to fix it.

Take time to be still and listen.

Reflective Ways to Worship

Reflective worship is done in silence and reflects upon God's presence in your life.

Silent Prayer

Take time to be still and listen. Give members time to silently commune with God. Start with just a minute or two, but eventually you may want to give members extended times to pray during group. You might even want to spend an entire group meeting in silent prayer. When you do this, give them permission to go off and find a place to be alone.

Moments of Solitude and Meditation

Meditate on passages of Scripture. Have a small group meeting during which members are asked to go away by themselves for an hour with their Bible. Perhaps provide them with paper and pen to write down their thoughts during this time of meditation. This can be done outside in a park setting or in a home by allowing members to go to different parts of the house. Then come back together and share with other members of the group—or don't. Another alternative is to gather for simple prayer and then release members while they are still in a contemplative mood.

Fasting

Encourage group members to go on a fast. Start small, maybe a meal or an activity to give back to God. Then you can build to a two- or three-day-long group fast—whether from food or an activity. Be available to support each other during the week via social media, emails, and phone calls. (For more information, go to www.smallgroups.net/fasting.)

Share God Stories

Have you ever thought about the Israelites and just wondered: Are these people just missing it or what? God parts the Red Sea for them. He gives them manna for breakfast. When they are bored with that, God provides quail. When they are in the desert and are thirsty, Moses hits a rock with a stick and water comes out. And in the midst of these miracles, they drift away from God and start complaining again, again, and again. I used to read those stories and wonder: Are these people clueless? If that were me, I would never forget God. But when I look back at my life and think about the times I have gotten discouraged, I realize that I also too quickly forget about the many times God met me in special ways, just as he did for the Israelites.

Ask your group members to tell each other how God is working in their life. Such stories can be a great way of not only adding depth to your relationships, but also of worshiping God for all he is doing. One of the best ways to encourage your group members to share their stories is by sharing yours with them. One of the stories I share is about a flashlight.

When I first became a Christian, my sister tried to teach me about tithing. I wasn't too sure about it. You know, when you are a teen and it is your older sister telling you something, you wonder if it's a scam.

At the time I had a paper route in order to earn some extra money. Every once in a while I took the money I earned on the paper route—which was paid mostly in change—to a local store to exchange the coins for paper money.

One of those times I gave the store clerk a bunch of coins and asked for ten dollars in return. As soon as he handed me the ten dollar bill, something felt different, but I put the money in my pocket and walked out the door. Once outside, I pulled the bill from my pocket and noticed that there were two ten-dollar bills stuck together!

I stood outside the store and wrestled with the decision. Should I just put the money back in my pocket, or should I return it? Then I heard a voice inside me saying, "Take the money back." For what seemed like an eternity, I stood outside that store and tried to decide. Finally, I walked back into the store and straight to the clerk. I handed the man the ten-dollar bill, saying, "Hey, two of these stuck together, and this one's yours." He had a perplexed look on his face, but I hurried out, not waiting around to get a reply.

A couple of weeks later I needed a flashlight and went back to the store. It wasn't until I was in the store that I realized I had forgotten my money. I figured I might as well look at the flashlights anyway. As I stood in front of those flashlights, without a dime in my pocket, I tell you God spoke to me. Not audibly, but very clearly I heard a voice telling me, "Pick up the flashlight."

I remember saying to God, "I don't have any money." But then I thought, *You know, what's the harm?* I wanted to be obedient, so I picked up the flashlight and walked toward the front of the store. I thought maybe someone had dropped some money on the floor and I would come across it on my way to the checkout. Maybe that's what God had in mind.

So I meandered to the checkout, looking for money on the floor. There was none.

I began to think perhaps someone in front of me in the checkout line would drop some money and I could pay for the flashlight that way. I stood in line as the people in front of me paid for their items and then walked out of the store. No one dropped a cent. I found myself standing in front of the checkout lady.

I was a very late bloomer growing up. Being shy and introverted, I just couldn't think of any words to say to the clerk. So I did the only thing I could think of doing and handed her the flashlight. She rang it up and told me the amount. I was so nervous that I just stood there and stared at her. Eventually she repeated the amount and told me that I had to pay her if I wanted the flashlight. But I just kept looking at her in silence, not knowing what to say or do—it was a very awkward moment. She repeated the amount once more, and my anxiety continued to build.

Then all of a sudden, from another part of the store I heard a man say, "That's the young man!" It caught me by surprise and sent a wave of panic through my body. I wasn't stealing the flashlight; I was just trying to buy it without money! The man walked around the corner and stood next to me. He spoke again, and I'll never forget the words he said as long as I live on this earth. "This is the young man who gave me the ten dollars back." He looked at the clerk and said to her, "Give him the flashlight."

God touches my life. He touches your life. He touches the lives of everyone in your small group.

In those moments when I am discouraged and I think I can't do ministry anymore, I remember not only that story but others like it. I have written them in a journal as reminders of God's love for me. These are stories about a living Savior—the God of Abraham, Jacob, and Isaiah—who touched my life. When I don't think I have the finances to pay for my kids' education or the expenses my son's special needs create, or when the load on our family seems too much, the God who prompted a man to turn to a clerk and say, "Give him the flashlight," is the same God who will meet my needs. He is the same God who will take care of my ministry. The same God who will take care of everything in the world.

God touches my life. He touches your life. He touches the lives of everyone in your small group. As the group leader, you need to remind your members of that and encourage them to share their God stories. And encourage them to share their dreams, because if they have a dream that is God-inspired, there is nothing that can stand in their way. If the God of the universe inspired that dream, he is telling you, "Pick up the flashlight." If you have the courage to obey and do what God says (buy the flashlight) then he will do his part.

Teach Group Members to Pray in Community

Praying is not easy for everyone. Praying *aloud* is easy for almost no one! There are some ways, however, that you can encourage your small group members to become more comfortable in praying within their community.

Start slowly and don't make people pray. Always give time for prayer in your small group meeting, but don't force the issue. As the leader, you may want to try this: Tell the group you are going to start the prayer and you will then give time for anyone else who wants to pray. When everyone who wants to is finished praying, you will close with prayer. As you start practicing this, you will have to be patient while waiting for others to speak. In the beginning, it's possible that no one will pray, but be patient and remain silent. Every group member in the room may be praying silently. The key is to model spoken prayer, give them time to do so, and then allow the Holy Spirit to work in your members. As you repeat this exercise every week, eventually more and more group members will feel comfortable enough to add their own prayers.

Model brief and simple prayers. Prayer time is *not* the time to try to impress anyone with your knowledge of biblical terms. Very often, those who are comfortable praying begin to extend the length of their prayers until they begin to sound like mini sermons instead of someone talking to God.

Prayer time is not the time to try to impress anyone with your knowledge of biblical terms.

Resist all urges to do so. Keep it simple because one of the best ways to encourage your group members to pray is by doing so in simple terms. And keep your own prayers short. If you have members who are hesitant to pray aloud, at the close of a group meeting you can tell everyone you are going to go around the room and ask everyone to offer a one-sentence prayer. Tell them that it must be one sentence only and it can be as simple as "Thank you." Lowering the bar like this lets group members know they are not expected to be great orators to talk to God.

Stop and pray right then and there. Be flexible in prayer. Always be willing to pray with people whenever God brings it up. If you're in group and somebody pours out their heart, be flexible and stop and pray right then and there. Don't wait until the end of the group and the *official* prayer time. Stopping to pray whenever needs arise conveys the message that *any* time is a good time to talk to God.

This story is from one of our small group leaders:

One of my small group members first joined us during the 40 Days of Purpose. He was not a Christian at the time (he has since come to Christ), and I'm sure he rarely ever prayed privately and certainly had never prayed publicly. In the course of life in our group, we began to model praying whenever situations came up. When someone shared a problem or concern in our group, we always stopped right then and prayed. This guy never wanted to pray aloud, but he watched the rest of us model that behavior. One day while he was going through a crisis at his business, he called me and said, "Hey, can we get the group together and just pray for what I'm going through?"

He didn't learn that because the group did a study on prayer. He learned that because his group modeled that behavior.

Your prayer time. What if you are the small group leader and *you* are the one who has a difficult time praying? Well if that is true, let me assure you that you are not alone. I remember the first time I had to pray aloud in a small group as a new Christian. Our leader always closed in prayer. One night he said, "We're going to close a little differently tonight." I knew the word *differently* could not be good. I was going to have to do something beyond sitting in silence with my eyes closed. I could feel the panic creeping through my body. My heart started beating rapidly. Then he said, "Let's go around the circle and each say a one-sentence prayer of closing." And I'm thinking, *Hey I did not sign up for this!* Then he pointed to the person on his right and said, "Please start the prayer."

I started thinking, *Five more people and I have to pray. Four more people and I have to pray. Three more people and I have to pray.* I wanted to run from the room. I wanted the world to end right then and there. *Christ, just call me home right now—I'm ready.* But the Rapture did not come, and I was praying aloud. I have no memory of what I said that day. Knowing me, I probably prayed for the food.

Anyway, my point is that my journey did not exactly start out bravely. The whole idea of praying aloud was terrifying to me. Who would have ever thought I would become a pastor? Not me!

When you are alone at home praying (or even in the car), instead of always praying silently, I encourage you to pray aloud. I have been a pastor since 1982—thirty years—but sometimes when I pray silently my mind starts drifting. It goes something like this, *Thank you, God, for this day and all of the people who touch my life. You have really touched my life, and . . . I can't believe the Broncos lost! What was up with that? Man, that ticks me off!* Before I know it I am doing a play-by-play of the game and have completely forgotten I was in the middle of a prayer. Eventually I'll catch myself and throw in an *Amen*, but it isn't ideal. Now, if I pray aloud, my mind stays focused and I can have a meaningful conversation with God. Something about speaking aloud to God connects me to him. Give it a try.

The deepest level of worship is praising God in spite of pain, trials, temptation, suffering, or distance from God. It is easy to worship God on Sunday morning when everything is going great in our lives and we like the song we are singing. It can be tougher when it seems as though everything in our life is going wrong and we don't even want to get out of bed to go to church. When you are able to worship God in those times, you begin to understand true worship.

How do you and your group worship in these less-than-ideal times? Encourage group members to tell God, and each other, exactly how they feel. He is not afraid of our emotions. In those tough times, focus on God and his unchanging nature. "You gave me life and showed me kindness, and in your care you watched over my life" (Job 10:12 NCV). When you or your group members are going through a crisis, pull together and focus on Christ, not the problem. Romans 12:15 tells us to "mourn with those who mourn." Sometimes this can be exactly what people in crisis need. Don't offer answers. Don't try to *fix* them or their problem. Mourn with them. Pray with and for them. Trust God to keep his promise. Remember what God has already done, and always praise him. When you feel abandoned by God yet continue to trust him, you worship him in the deepest way possible.

When you feel abandoned by God yet continue to trust him, you worship him in the deepest way possible.

Surrender

The heart of worship is daily surrender to God. If I had to describe worship in a single word, that word would be *surrender*. Learning to worship God and place him first in our life requires learning how to surrender every area of our life. This means having the same level of commitment to God whether we are in church, at the office, in a factory, at a sporting event, or at home. Many people have several personas—one for church, one for work, one for leisure, one for home, and very often, one we never let anyone see. The heart of worship is surrendering every aspect of our life until our every act and thought glorifies God.

Is that an easy process? No. And it won't happen all at once. Surrendering is not just a daily exercise. It happens hourly, and very often, by the minute. Every minute of our lives we have the potential to make a decision that honors God or one that moves away from him. The choice is ongoing, and it is always ours to make. Each one of us has to decide whether to make decisions that honor God. If we do, it shows our love for him; it is worship in the most fundamental sense of the word.

The heart of worship is surrendering every aspect of our life until our every act and thought glorifies God.

Romans 12:1–2 talks about being a living sacrifice. If we lay our life on the altar and God holds the knife, we need to trust that he is a surgeon, not an assassin. If we willingly stay on the altar, he will cut the sin out of our life, not kill us. Surrender and trust; go hand-in-hand with God.

Obedience and Trust

Surrender is best demonstrated in obedience and trust. Obeying God when it does not make sense is at the heart of surrender. Once you as the small group leader understand this simple fact of faith, you can begin to model and encourage it in your group members. Whenever a group member has a decision to make, always encourage him or her to seek the answer directly from God. Prayer, waiting in silence for an answer, and following obediently is our purest form of surrender. In community, the test of faith in trust through surrender is doable.

Ongoing Support

Having a small group of Christians to support us in our ongoing surrender is vital. If we are going to stay surrendered, we need to have some people in our life who will provide accountability and support. We were never meant to go it alone as Christians. From the beginning, God's plan was for us to live and worship in community. That has not changed. When Christ was asked what was the greatest commandment of all, his answer was, "Love the Lord your God with all your heart and with all your soul and with all your mind and with all your strength" (Mark 12:30). Loving with *all* of our soul, mind, and strength will require the support of other Christians.

Disclosure with Someone Else

Full surrender requires disclosure with someone we trust. Sometimes we have issues we do not want to share with the entire group. One of the best ways for group members to feel comfortable sharing such issues is to encourage them to have a spiritual partner (of the same sex). As mentioned earlier, a spiritual partner is someone who knows the areas of our life that need to be surrendered. They can come alongside us and ask, "How is it going? How can I help you?" Ideally, group members will find spiritual partners within the group, but the most important thing is that every person has someone they can trust to go to with their struggles and problems.

Worship looks different to each of us. As group leader, your responsibility is to recognize that fact and encourage group members to try various venues and methods of worship. Help them realize that worship is more than just music and is a direct reflection of our love for God.

────────── **ACTION STEPS** ──────────

1. What is one *expressive* way you can worship in your small group?

   _____

   _____

   _____

2. What is one *reflective* way you can worship in your small group?

   _____

   _____

   _____

3. What is one of your God stories that you can share with your group? Commit to sharing that story with your group during the next month.

   _____

   _____

   _____

14

Worship—Practical Suggestions

How to Experience God Moments

Love the LORD your God with all your heart and with all your soul and with all your strength.

Deuteronomy 6:5

A person will worship something, have no doubt about that. We may think our tribute is paid in secret in the dark recesses of our hearts, but it will [come] out. That which dominates our imaginations and our thoughts will determine our lives, and our character. Therefore, it behooves us to be careful what we worship, for what we are worshipping we are becoming.

Ralph Waldo Emerson

Worship is commonly neglected in small groups because people often equate worship with singing. Worship is much more than merely music. The following are some practical ideas for worship. They are categorized under crawl, walk, and run.

Crawl

Break into prayer groups of three or four. Think of specific people who serve in your church and pray for God's blessing on their lives.

Pray for people who have wandered from the faith. James 5:19 says, "If you know people who have wandered off from God's truth, don't write them off. . . . Get them back" (Message). Break into prayer groups of three or four people and pray for those you know who have wandered from the faith. Ask God to show you if there is anything you can do to bring them back.

Write a letter to God. What do you want to say to God as your best friend? Take a moment to write out a brief prayer expressing your desire to pursue a friendship with God.

Sentence prayers. As discussed in the previous chapter, praying aloud in a group is very difficult for some people. To make it a bit easier, try one-sentence prayers. Tell group members, "We are going to go around the room and offer God one-sentence prayers. No longer. It can be as simple as 'Thank you' or a bit longer. But remember, keep it to one sentence." Not only does this make it easier for reluctant group members to offer a simple prayer, but it also keeps the more verbose members from monopolizing prayer time.

Pray in trios. During prayer time, break into groups of three and spend a bit more time sharing your prayer requests with each other. Before returning to the rest of the group, be sure to take turns praying for each individual in your group of three.

I love this church! As a group, make a list of things you love about your church. Then spend some time thanking God for bringing you to such a church. Then ask group members:

195

"What one thing could we do to make our church even better?" Once you come up with an answer, decide how your group can make that happen.

Traits of God. Bring a poster board to the group meeting and ask members to brainstorm and come up with character traits of God (forgiving, loving, and so forth). After you have listed all of the traits you can think of, spend some time in prayer and thanksgiving for these traits.

A night of worship. Ask group members to bring their favorite worship song (on CD or DVD) to the next group meeting. During that meeting, play each person's song and ask the person to share what that song means to him or her.

Set the mood. Treat your group prayer time as something special—which it is! Spend a moment to dim the lighting, light some candles, or play quiet instrumental music in the background. This can be a great way to focus members and remind them of the importance of prayer.

Walk

Pray by social media, email, or phone. Challenge group members to engage someone they have not talked with in a while. As the thread of conversation draws to a close, ask that person if they can pray for him or her. And then do so right then and there. Social media, email, and phone can be a great tool for reaching out to people. It is nonthreatening (as opposed to a surprise visit, for example) and only takes a few moments out of their day and yours. This even works for texting. Just text a prayer—after all, who wouldn't want a prayer texted to them?

Surrender an unhealthy habit. Rick says, "To avoid being stung, stay away from bees." As an act of worship and because it will please the Lord, what is an outside influence you are willing to give up that contributes to a persistent temptation (for example, a soap opera or other TV show,

R-rated movies, a magazine subscription, a place you visit, an unhealthy relationship)?

Speak prayers of praise and thanksgiving. Worshiping God is one way of fixing your eyes on what is eternal. Take some time as a group to speak out prayers of praise and thanksgiving to God. This is a challenging exercise in prayer. Don't ask God for anything yet; just praise him for who he is and for what he has done.

Share God stories with each other. During your worship time invite group members to share a *God story.* This is a story of a way the supernatural God intersected their life in a miraculous way.

Keep a group prayer journal. Ask someone in your group to collect the group prayers in a journal. As they are answered, mark them in a special way—perhaps put a small heart next to them as a symbol of God's love. Encourage group members to be creative and have fun. Then spend just a few minutes of every meeting asking if any prayers have been answered and asking for new prayer requests. This is a great way to see God at work in your group.

> *Worshiping God is one way of fixing your eyes on what is eternal.*

Beautiful words. Spend a meeting asking group members to read a favorite passage from the Bible. Let them know ahead of time that you will be doing this exercise so they have plenty of time to choose a passage and prepare. After each person reads, have a few moments of silence for members to use in whatever way they see fit. Perhaps they may choose to reflect silently on the meaning of the words, pray for the person who read them, thank God for the words found in that passage, or just sit quietly and ask God to speak to them in the silence. The idea is to allow the Word of God to prompt members into worshiping him in whatever way fits their personality.

Be a living sacrifice. As a group, read Romans 12:1, "Therefore, I urge you, brothers, in view of God's mercy, to offer your bodies as a living sacrifice, holy and pleasing to

God—this is your spiritual act of worship." Discuss what this means. How can we be living sacrifices? How can we be holy and pleasing to God? How can our lives reflect our love of God? Specifically, in what ways can we offer ourselves as holy sacrifices?

Back to the hymns. Choose a well-known hymn ("Amazing Grace," "How Great Thou Art," "To God Be the Glory," etc.) and print out the lyrics. During your next group meeting, play the song and ask group members what the words to the song mean to them. Play the song again and ask members to listen carefully while remembering what other group members said about the song. Use the time to allow God to reach you through both the music and the words of others.

In the name of God. Bring a poster board to the group meeting and ask members to brainstorm and come up with all of the names for God that they can think of (Abba, Lord, Shepherd, etc.). Once you have come up with a list, go around the room and ask group members to identify the name that they most identify with God. Ask them to tell the group what that name signifies about their relationship with God.

Worship together. Encourage group members to attend the same service and worship together. Experiencing worship together is a great way to bond. You may want to all go out to lunch together, but be sure to stress that the lunch is completely optional and not expected. Group members may not be able to afford lunch for the entire family or may have other family-oriented plans. Be flexible and have fun.

Run

Flames of surrender. Spend a group meeting gathered in front of a fireplace or an outdoor fire pit. Supply group members with paper and pencil and ask them to write down anything they are having a difficult time surrendering to God. After they have written it down, ask them to fold it a couple of times (so that it is not visible), and then ask everyone to spend some time in silent prayer, asking God to help them surrender this area of their life. When everyone has finished praying, drop the pieces of paper into the flames and watch them disappear.

Scripture memorization. Challenge group members to memorize one verse of the Bible every week. Suggest they write it down on an index card and put it in a place where they will see it often, such as the bathroom mirror, on the kitchen counter, or on their bedside table. Periodically ask group members to recite one of their memorized verses during a group meeting.

Prayer during the service. If your church has multiple services, attend one service as a group, and then during the next service, retreat to a room to pray for the pastor as he speaks. Contact your church ahead of time and ask where the group can meet. If you don't have multiple services, your group may want to simply arrive early and spend ten minutes right before the service praying for the pastor. Depending on how your church is set up, you could do this right in the sanctuary or in an empty room in the church.

Confess your sins. James 5:16 tells us, "Confess your sins to each other and pray for each other so that you may be healed. The earnest prayer of a righteous person has great power and wonderful results" (NLT). Read this passage aloud during a group meeting and then spend some time discussing it. Go around the room and ask group members what this passage means to them. Have they ever confessed their sins to someone? How did it go? Why does God want us to confess our sins to each other when we can confess them directly to him? Then ask group members to risk stepping out of their comfort zone and confess a sin to the entire group. Everyone has some sort of sin they are dealing with. As each individual does so, spend a few minutes praying for him or her.

Share your talent. Ask if anyone in the group plays a musical instrument. If so, encourage him or her to bring the

199

instrument to an upcoming group session to play during a time of worship.

Communion. If your church allows you, as a small group leader, to lead communion, spend a group meeting taking communion together. In a small group, you can take time to pass out the bread and discuss the act of taking communion. Encourage group members to ask for prayer if it is needed.

Ask group members to risk stepping out of their comfort zone and confess a sin to the entire group.

You may want to spend some time sharing the story of how you first came to believe in Christ. After you take the juice or wine, give everyone time to reflect and think about the importance of this tradition.

Meditate on Scripture. Spend a group meeting meditating on a biblical passage. Read it aloud, one sentence at a time, giving group members time to reflect on these holy words. End with prayer.

Moments of solitude. Surprise your group members by announcing that this meeting will be spent in solitude. Be sure everyone has a Bible, some paper, a pen for journaling (optional), and a place to go. You may want to divide up into different rooms of the house, or if weather permits, send some people outside. Spend an hour alone with God. After that hour, come back together as a group and share about your experience.

Foot washing. Foot washing may not be something you want to try with a brand new group, but in a group that has been meeting for a while, this can be a very powerful moment in the life of a group. Keep it simple and beautiful. Provide small hand towels and ask group members to pair up. Light some candles and play soft music. Although members may be a little tense at first, do your best to make this a solemn experience by setting the tone yourself. Volunteer to go first, and as you perform the act, think of Christ doing the same for his disciples. As you wash the person's feet, ask how you can pray for him or her.

──────────── **ACTION STEPS** ────────────

1. What step from this chapter can you implement in your group?

   _____

   _____

   _____

2. Who can help you implement the step?

   _____

   _____

   _____

3. When will you do it?

   _____

   _____

   _____

Keeping Your Group Focused

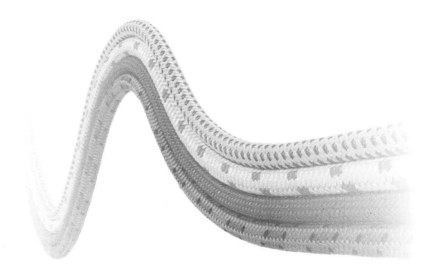

15

How to Keep Your Group on Track

Obstacles and Opportunities for Growth

Get rid of all bitterness, rage and anger, brawling and slander, along with every form of malice. Be kind and compassionate to one another, forgiving each other, just as in Christ God forgave you.

Ephesians 4:31–32

Difficulties are meant to rouse, not discourage. The human spirit is to grow strong by conflict.

William Ellery Channing

No problems? If you are a strong and wise leader you will never have any problems with the members of your small group, right? Wrong! The only way you will never have problems in your small group is if you are the only person in your small group. Whenever you get two or more people together, conflict is likely. Put eight or ten people in a room together and conflict is inevitable.

Preventing Conflict

As the leader of a small group, your job is to be prepared for any conflict that arises. Knowing ahead of time what types of conflict are most likely and how to handle them will make you a more effective leader and lighten your stress load.

Childcare

Although this problem was addressed in some detail at the beginning of chapter 4, you need to be aware that it will be an ongoing issue and be prepared to handle it. Don't let members use a lack of childcare as an excuse for dropping out of your small group. (See pages 78–79.)

Setting up the Home

Setting up the home environment is important. Factors to consider include:

If you have pets, make sure they do not disturb the group time. Make sure people in the group have no allergies to the pets you have. If anyone does, ask for volunteers with no pets to offer their home as a meeting place.

Lighting is important. You don't want it so cozy that you don't have enough light to read.

Monitor the temperature. Pay attention to those around you and determine if they are too hot or too cold.

Provide places for people to set drinks if you will have them where you study.

Decide on your group guidelines (see pages 207–8) so everyone is on the same page.

Cell phone courtesy is a must because it can be a distraction (including texts, emails, Facebook, and Twitter). Arrange the seats so that everyone can see each other. A circle works best to encourage conversation. If there is a new person, be sure to have name tags for everyone.

First Impressions

The first impression is usually a lasting one, so you want it to be a positive one. To make this happen, you can work in three zones:

1. *Before the group meets*—Connect with those who are coming for the first time. Make sure they have directions, ask if there is anything you can do to accommodate any special needs, but most of all, make sure they know you are excited about them coming.
2. *During the group time*—Be sure to greet them using their first name. Be mindful that if you are a hugger, not everyone else is; you have to earn the right to give hugs. Make sure they are included in the group conversation. If they don't participate, ask if there is anything they would like to add. Be yourself so they can be themselves; and smile. And make sure you start and end on time.
3. *After the meeting*—Let them know that you appreciate them coming. Find out if there is anything they would change or add to make for a great experience. Also, ask them to bring a bag of chips or veggies to the next group meeting—there is nothing like a small responsibility to help them feel valued.

Group Guidelines

Group guidelines are just that—a guide to help you have a great group. They help communicate values and details to which the group agrees. For an example of Saddleback's small group guidelines, go to www.smallgroups.net/gg. There you can download a free sample to see what we do. In the values portion we share nine areas to agree on that are important to Saddleback Church. In the details portion you make decisions about specifics related to just your group. During over twenty years of managing groups in churches, I have found one thing in common among groups that have conflicts or problems: they don't have group guidelines.

How Do I Navigate a Lesson?

The lesson is a tool to prompt discussion and learning; adapt it to the needs of your group. Remember, you don't have to answer all the questions. Most curriculums have more questions than you can answer. So a few days before the group meeting, read them over to decide which questions your group needs to discuss. Spending quality time on a few questions is better than skimming through all the questions. The lesson should be used to help spark the cognitive side of spiritual formation in each member.

Discussion

Having good discussion is the key for any group to thrive and move to the next level. To start any discussion, people have to feel safe talking. Most curriculums will start with an icebreaker. This may seem trivial, and you may want to skip it for the sake of time, but icebreakers are critical to getting conversation going. They will give you the opportunity to learn new things about the people you are with that the study wouldn't necessarily bring up.

Most study questions are designed with *what* and *how* questions to get people to share. Try to involve as many people as possible because when people discuss and ask further questions, you learn where they are in their spiritual development and life in general. Know what you want to accomplish in the study so you can gauge how much discussion is on target and how much is more like rabbit trails. Any discussion is a balance between Holy Spirit moments and people just rambling. Be sensitive to the difference between God doing something you may not have planned and the group going off course. Before the group meeting starts, know the one thing you want to accomplish so you can feel comfortable if the group doesn't get through all the questions.

During over twenty years of managing groups in churches, I have found one thing in common among groups that have conflicts or problems: they don't have group guidelines.

Listening Well

How do you listen well? It starts by looking at the person talking. Don't stare him or her down eyeball to eyeball, but look at the zone between the eyebrows to the tip of the nose. And pay attention! Listen with your eyes. Ears are important, but when your eyes are engaged, you stay focused. If your study guide or cell phone tends to be a distraction, set it aside. Then ask follow-up questions to be sure you understand the person's perspective. Don't try to change his or her perspective, instead seek to understand first.

Curriculum Diet

What you study is just as important as *having* a study. You want to make sure that throughout the year your group gets a good balance of books of the Bible, doctrine, topical studies, and life skills. (See our Small Group Curriculum Pathway Ideas at www.smallgroups.net/resources for suggestions for your group.)

Making Prayer Work

My real friends don't have to ask what to pray for because they know what's going on in my life. That's an awesome place to be! As community deepens in your group, you will start to recognize prayer needs. Until that happens, however, start with these guidelines:

Write down the requests. You may use a journal, or maybe you have a private group on your social media. The bottom line is to use whatever you need to keep track of your group members' requests.

Give an appropriate amount of time to actually pray for the requests.

Encourage a group atmosphere in which stopping immediately and praying for a need isn't awkward.

Coach your members to be as specific as possible.

Look for a variety of ways to incorporate prayer into your group time. Sometimes break up by gender to pray, other times break into groups of two or three, or sometimes ask one person to close in prayer. Be creative and ask others to give suggestions.

After your group has been together for a while, look for the depth of requests. If after three to six months together the group members are still not opening up and making requests concerning more personal issues in their lives, your group may have a safety issue. It may be a good time to discuss whether people feel safe giving specific, personal prayer requests.

If after three to six months together the group members are still not opening up and making requests concerning more personal issues in their lives, your group may have a safety issue.

Sample Group Evening Timeline

Although no two small groups are the same, here are some things to consider. Start with a time of introducing each other when someone is new, or catch up on what's new with each other since you were together. This may stir up some times for prayer or maybe a completely different group time than planned.

Next, get into your Bible study (curriculum). You are at the group to learn and apply. These two components make up holistic discipleship! Generally this time is devoted mostly to learning; however, you may discover that the "applying what you learned" part may need a different time to make this a reality. Remember, both need to happen.

Finally, close with heart. Don't rush the close, but be strategic and aware of final things you need to say to the group before the next time. Always make your next step in the current step. In other words, use the close to solidify action steps (what you're doing—applying, sharing prayer requests and commitments, etc.) and wrap up what has taken place while you've been together.

The Meeting after the Meeting

You need to make sure you end your group meeting on time. This is a small group's formal time. After you end the meeting, those who need to leave will leave, but some will stay. We call this *the meeting after the meeting*. Although it is not a formal meeting and no curriculum is used, this time is valuable in learning where people are in their personal lives, and often ministry opportunities present themselves. Be aware that sometimes the most important group time is after the formal meeting ends.

The Other 166 Hours

Outside the formal time when your group meets, such as Thursday evenings from 7:00 to 9:00, there are another 166 hours each week that you can use to help form community faster and deeper. This informal group time can be anything you do together, including coffee times, parties, seminars you attend together, your kids' activities, group service projects, missions trips, and so on. Think of ways you can use the informal times to help your group grow deeper. The techniques you use to build a friendship can be used for group building.

How Do I Grow My Group?

Be more concerned about spiritual growth than numeric growth. As long as your group has three people, it's the three God wants you to pour into. As you work on spiritual health through balancing the five biblical purposes, spiritual health will bring numerical growth.

What if the Group Doesn't Work?

If your group doesn't work after you have given it a four- to six-week run, it's not the end of the world. Learn from it and ask other successful groups what it was they did to have success. Just because it may not have gelled together this time doesn't mean the next group won't work. Grab a couple of friends who want to commit to community and give it another chance.

Should We Meet during the Summer?

A better question is, why do you meet? What is the purpose of your group meeting? At Saddleback our groups are developing health through the context of relationship and friendship. For my group, summer is the best run our group has because our time is not taken up with sports activities for our kids and helping with homework. Although people take vacations during the summer, most are not gone longer than two weeks. So even if they miss a couple of times, the rest of the group can still meet. If you meet for spiritual health, it's a year-round gig. Are there times for different frequency? Sure. But I would not stop for a few months. I don't take a break from my marriage for the summer. Why? Because staying with it keeps it healthy.

Conflict Resolution

Follow biblical principles for conflict resolution. It's important to immediately resolve any conflicts or concerns by following the principles of Matthew 18:15–17:

> If your brother sins against you, go and show him his fault, just between the two of you. If he listens to you, you have won your brother over. But if he will not listen, take one or two others along, so that "every matter may be established by the testimony of two or three witnesses." If he refuses to listen to them, tell it to the church; and if he refuses to listen even to the church, treat him as you would a pagan or a tax collector.

When Sally, a small group member, comes to the host and says, "I've got a problem with Jane," the host's first response should be, "Have you discussed it with her?" If she hasn't, the host needs to say, "I don't want to hear about it until you've had an opportunity to discuss it with her."

When you have conflict in your group, it's not a bad thing; it's simply a warning light telling you your group needs attention.

Conflict is like the lights on the dashboard of your car. When the warning lights come on, your car needs attention. When you have conflict in your group, it's not a bad thing; it's simply a warning light telling you your group needs attention. Most often it is an issue of character, resulting in poor communication.

ABCs of Conflict Resolution

At Saddleback we have come up with an acronym to help us remember how to handle conflict resolution:

A—Ask God for direction.
B—Be praying for the people involved.
C—Care enough to confront.

A good book that takes this subject further is *The Peacemaker* by Ken Sande.

Late People

There is only one thing worse than people who are always late, and that is people who are always late and are noisy when they arrive. The group has already started and you are in the middle of a conversation, but they don't notice. They arrive flustered and with a litany of excuses. "Sorry I'm late, but I was ready to leave and I couldn't find my book. And then my daughter-in-law called and I couldn't get off the phone. My grandson has the flu. . . ."

When this happens, you need to stress with the entire group the importance of arriving on time. Then add, "If you have to be late, remember that the group will still start promptly, so please come in quietly and find a seat without disturbing the group." If their late arrivals continue, you will need to talk to them privately and explain that their behavior is disruptive to the group. Ask what you can do to facilitate them arriving on time, and offer to meet at their house if that will help.

Talkative People

The talkative person seldom realizes he or she is talking too much. The individual has a comment for every question and every situation. If you are not careful, that person will dominate the group and give others little time to speak.

If Jerry is the talkative one, avoid making eye contact with him when you ask the group questions. Be intentional in asking others to speak. If necessary, speak to him privately, outside of group time. Do so gently, however. Tell him you appreciate his contributions, and ask him to help you get others to contribute in the same way. You can also ask Jerry to sit next to you so that if he is talking too much, you can set up a signal (like a nudge) to help him be more aware of his tendency.

Quiet People

If you have a quiet person in the group who seldom contributes, you may need to intentionally work on getting him or her involved. Every so often turn to the individual and say, "Hey, I know you have good ideas. Do you want to weigh in on this?" Give the individual permission and opportunity to speak. If you don't, the more dominant people in the group will take more than their share of time during the discussion period. Subgrouping (pages 159–61) is another great way to help quiet people feel comfortable enough to talk.

Poor Attendance

Vacations, life events, and family emergencies happen. It is almost impossible to have perfect small group attendance, particularly if you are in a group that has met together for years. If your group continues to meet during the summer months, family vacations will inevitably increase absenteeism. Give grace during such periods. Continue meeting, even if only a few of you can attend. Remember, God is always with you, so there is no such thing as a wasted meeting.

In the case of someone who has regularly poor attendance with no real excuse, privately speak to the person and ask if there is a problem. Very often it is a matter of scheduling. If this is the case, suggest the person join another group that would be more conducive to his or her schedule.

Remember, God is always with you, so there is no such thing as a wasted meeting.

Emphasize that the person will be missed, but the important thing is for him or her to get into a group where it is possible to make it to the meetings with regularity.

Gossip

If you're not familiar with Matthew 18:15–17, you need to memorize that Scripture because small groups are a playground

215

for the enemy to bring up all kinds of things like divisiveness, heresy and doctrinal issues, and gossip. Gossip is probably one of the greatest tools that the enemy has in his arsenal. And what I encourage you to do is understand what gossip is. This is my quick teaching on gossip: If you are not part of the problem or part of the solution, you need to shut up.

If someone says, "You know, I probably shouldn't share this, but . . . ," as the leader you need to stop right there and say, "Don't share it." Are you part of the problem or part of the solution?

If you are not part of the problem or part of the solution, you need to shut up.

Another possible danger comes during prayer time. Someone says, "I'd like to pray for Bill and Sally because I think there's something going on between the two of them, and so, could we just pray for them, because I think they're doing, you know, things, so let's just pray for them." That wasn't a prayer request; that was gossip time.

So you need to teach your group on these issues. If you have a problem, you go to that person. If he or she doesn't listen to you, bring someone else with you. If the person still doesn't listen to you, bring the church into it. But be careful to understand and practice the biblical way to confront.

Members Who Never Do the Homework

There will be times when members do not get the assigned reading done. Life happens and that is to be expected. Encourage group members to attend the meetings even if they have not been able to finish their homework. Give plenty of grace in that area. The discussions are always important to build relationships, even if not every member has read the material.

If a particular group member continually shows up unprepared, however, it may be a sign of a deeper problem. Take some time to connect with that person and find out what is going on in his or her life.

Alcohol

Any time you serve alcohol, it is a danger. Biblically, it's fine. There's nothing wrong with having a drink. The problem is that sometimes groups don't know when to say *when*. This can prove to be a stumbling block to somebody who is a recovering alcoholic. We like to play it safe and say, "Let's limit our freedom for the benefit of others." If you need alcohol to have fun in your group, then you need a new group. "Therefore let us stop passing judgment on one another. Instead, make up your mind not to put any stumbling block or obstacle in your brother's way" (Rom. 14:13).

Caring for ECRs[1]

In the life of any small group, there will come a time when the small group leader will have concerns and struggles regarding how to handle difficult people in their group. Every small group is composed of many different personalities, and the small group leader must have a firm handle on how to identify and care for each of those personalities. Those group members who present special challenges we call ECRs: Extra Care Required. If not handled properly, an ECR can destroy a group.

Every small group is composed of many different personalities, and the small group leader must have a firm handle on how to identify and care for each of those personalities.

Evidently, ECRs existed in biblical times too. The apostle Paul describes three distinct ECR personalities, and he also offers the remedies for caring for these individuals: "And we urge you, brethren, admonish the *unruly*, encourage the *fainthearted*, help the *weak*, be patient with all men" (1 Thess. 5:14 NASB, italics mine).

---

1. This section on ECRs is heavily influenced by two men who shaped my thinking on the matter—Carl George and Dale Galloway.

Type 1 ECRs, the Unruly—Admonish Them

Unruly group members seem to have a knack for drawing the life out of every group they attend. Week after week they use small group as a therapy couch, lamenting about all of the problems in their life (which never seem to improve). This type of ECR is completely unaware of how much of the small group's time they are actually consuming. Upon closer observation, the unruly ECRs can be most properly labeled, "in need of attention."

Character traits of unruly ECRs are:

needy
controlling
loud
nonrepentant
opinionated
conflict-driven

Caring for the unruly ECR:
What they need most is to be challenged.

1. Understand they are under attack from Satan.
2. Pray for them to understand and fulfill their potential.
3. Understand the art of confrontation and how you can balance love and grace by following the principles in Matthew 18:15–17.
4. Attempt to make them an ally. ("Help me get others to share as you do.")
5. Speak privately with them about their need to consume the group's time.
6. Caution them that continued disruptive behavior will result in their removal from the group.
7. Control the time given to each person to share. ("Each of us will have one minute to share on this issue.")

Type 2 ECRs, the Fainthearted—Encourage Them

Fainthearted ECRs will most likely resemble the *church mouse* within the setting of their small group. These ECRs may have recently started to take spiritual inventory and are beginning to make life changes in how they think about God. They may spend months just attending, listening, and taking it all in. Fainthearted ECRs may not be used to sharing their faith or praying with other believers, and they will probably feel threatened if the small group leader puts them on the spot to share anything.

Character traits of fainthearted ECRs are:

quiet
guarded
fearful
timid
lacking self-esteem
wary
under construction in their faith

Caring for the fainthearted ECR:
What they need most is to be encouraged.

1. Pray specifically that God will begin encouraging them to open up over time. Until then, be patient.
2. Understand that God is using the small group to help them build their faith.
3. Encourage them in saying their attendance is important and appreciated.
4. Be careful not to put them on the spot during sharing time.
5. Gently assure them that God is in control of their life.
6. Find a positive trait in their personality and character and build on it.
7. Affirm them sincerely any time they share.

Type 3 ECRs, the Weak—Help Them

Weak ECRs are quite often the ones struggling to *get off the mat* in their lives. The storms of life have blown harshly. Many Christian ECRs in this category may have recently had a death in the family, lost a job, or even have lost everything due to a substance abuse problem. They come to the group bewildered and wonder if God really cares for them. Many ECRs in this category are living day-to-day with economic and emotional pressures. If the truth were known, these ECRs would tell you that they are just trying to survive. Another ECR in this category is the unbeliever who is attempting to get closer to God but is finding it difficult because of an addictive, sinful lifestyle.

Character traits of weak ECRs:

> coming out of tragedy
> lack of faith
> destructive life patterns
> highly sensitive
> in bondage to a sinful lifestyle
> barely surviving
> noncommittal

Caring for the weak ECRs:
What they need most is to be helped and carried.

1. Give them extra personal touches (letters, phone calls).
2. Love and affirm them.
3. Never ignore them.
4. Take them by the hand.
5. Counsel them to take life one day at a time.
6. Provide specific guidance.
7. Give them grace and gifts from their small group when appropriate.

8. Recognize their extreme levels of patience and understanding as a positive trait but also protect them from being taken advantage of in this area.

On Suffering

The Bible tells us that suffering is the product of a broken and fallen world. But as believers, we are blessed to have a unique perspective. Romans 12 provides some insight into how we should be dealing with suffering. In Romans 12:12, we read, "Be joyful in hope, patient in affliction, faithful in prayer." Romans 12:15 tells us, "Rejoice with those who rejoice; mourn with those who mourn." As a small group leader, please remember that it is not your job to "fix" those who are suffering. Instead, mourn with them. Be ready to listen.

Here's what Paul says: "Consider it pure joy, my brothers, whenever you face trials of many kinds" (James 1:2). That means to rejoice. How can we rejoice, and why should we?

First, we are not to be surprised by suffering. "Dear friends, do not be surprised at the painful trial you are suffering, as though something strange were happening to you" (1 Peter 4:12). We are not immune from it. "For it has been granted to you on behalf of Christ not only to believe on him, but also to suffer for him" (Phil. 1:29). Because we are Christians, God will use our suffering for a holy purpose. "And we know that in all things God works for the good of those who love him, who have been called according to his purpose" (Rom. 8:28).

Second, in Romans 5:8, Paul tells us that suffering is proof positive of the great love God has for us: "But God demonstrates his own love for us in this: While we were still sinners, Christ died for us." And in Romans 5:3–5, Paul reveals one of the most powerful products of suffering: "We also rejoice in our sufferings, because we know that suffering produces perseverance; perseverance, character; and character, hope. And hope does not disappoint us, because God has poured out his love into our hearts by the Holy Spirit, whom he has given us." Hope gives us the confidence to stand boldly in the face of the world and declare that there *is* hope even in the midst of suffering. We are living witnesses that Christ is the hope of the world, that even in the midst of troubles that face everyone on this broken planet, we can say with confidence through faith that God is bringing good out of that hardship.

And finally, we have the assurance of God's eternal reward. James says, "Blessed is the man who perseveres under trial, because when he has stood the test, he will receive the crown of life that God has promised to those who love him" (James 1:12). We need to expect suffering not only in our own lives but also in the lives of others. As a leader, be patient and faithful in both circumstances.

How long should suffering last? Only God knows that answer. But we are blessed to have faith in the outcome!

For more information on obstacles and opportunities for growth, visit www.smallgroups.net/faq.

──────────── ACTION STEPS ────────────

1. What are two or three areas in which your group can improve?

   _____

   _____

   _____

2. As a group, how can you commit to improving in these areas?

   _____

   _____

   _____

3. If it will help, put it into writing in your group guidelines and ask the entire group to agree and commit to the guidelines.

_____

_____

_____

4. Send your obstacle or opportunity for growth to info@smallgroups.net so we can add it to www.small groupnetwork.com.

16

It Continues with You!

How God Uses Ordinary People in Extraordinary Ways

He must become greater; I must become less.

John 3:30

People see WHAT you do; God sees WHY you do it.

Anonymous

As I lead the small group ministry at Saddleback Church, I am amazed at how God has used ordinary people in extraordinary ways.

Look at the disciples. He took ordinary men and used them in extraordinary ways. They weren't the "pretty" people of the time, the rich and famous, or the most biblically literate. They were willing not only to start the journey with Jesus, but to continue through the ups and downs and remain steadfast to the very end.

As someone who is in a small group and has been for over three decades, I know that starting in a small group with other people is the easy part. The hard part is sticking with it through the messy times. But that's where I've come to understand that God has a plan, and even though the plan isn't scripted the way I want, I stay the course.

Many times over the last ten years with our current small group, it would have been easy to leave and get another group started. But because we stayed (and so did they), we have seen God turn disasters into moments where his mercy and grace show up. Our fellowship is richer, our discipleship is deeper, our service in ministry is developing, our worship is transparent, and our evangelism is exciting. We have been able to speak into each other's lives because we spent the time to build trust and tell the truth. You can't get that from a group that has been together less than a year.

Close friends of ours have had a similar experience in their group. Read this legacy of Butch and Lisa's group:

Lisa and I started our small group in 1993 with other young married couples when our first child, Christian, was born. We've shared the seasons of raising families and supporting each other in the community of small group life.

During the past eighteen years, our group has experienced all life's realities: illnesses, job losses, financial issues, loss of family members, infertility, and many other challenges. We've also experienced rich joy sharing many abundant blessings. Our small group has been a source of God's strength as we've prayed and cared for each other through all the circumstances we face together. Small group life truly has served the purpose of helping each other grow closer to Christ as we grow closer together, experiencing the Great Commission and Great Commandment. God faithfully uses everything for good!

This year one of our original members, Kevin Wilson, was called home to heaven after a long fight with muscular dystrophy. Once again our small group was there, this time for his wife, Karen. Through our support and prayers, Karen was able to make a very hard decision with the doctors to remove life support and place Kevin in God's hands. When life brings an experience like this, a small group family is essential for prayer, love, and support.

Lisa and I were very honored when Karen asked us to host Kevin's memorial service with our small group. We prayed and shared how each of us was blessed to have shared our lives with Kevin. It was also a wonderful reunion with members who have started their own small groups. Since Kevin was previously in the music ministry, Rick Muchow [Saddleback's worship pastor] attended and shared a prayer. Kevin's family and friends were very touched as they clearly saw the value of our small group in Kevin's and Karen's lives.

Our group of young married couples is rapidly becoming empty nesters as our children are beginning to leave for college. But we will continue to support each other in the future seasons of life. Kevin was the first of our group to go home. His purpose was complete, and we will one day join him. Until that day, our small group helps us to fulfill the purpose we each have.

Thank you, Steve, for all you are doing to support the small group ministry at Saddleback! I hope this testimony encourages you and others on the value of small groups in our church family.

So where are you on the journey of leading your small group? Whether you are thinking about a new person or a seasoned veteran leading a group, one thing is guaranteed: Satan doesn't want you applying the principles in this book. He will do all he can to make you feel insecure and fearful, not wanting your group to continue. Why? Because he doesn't want the Great Commission and Great Commandment happening. He doesn't want you developing your leadership gifts. He wants you ineffective. He will use all he can to keep you from being focused and purposeful.

But through every up and down, your group will grow stronger. Read this testimony from an email to our small group ministry:

> In terms of our group, I wrote to you in March because we had a profound tragedy. Elisa's husband, Bruce (also a group member), died tragically in a plane crash. None of us knew how to react or what to do. You gave us some amazing advice about things to say and not to say, and we took it to heart.
>
> We met the first week without Elisa, and all of us felt pretty useless and insecure. We didn't know if our group would really be what Elisa needed. We didn't know if she would feel comfortable or if we would know what to say or do. We didn't know if she would even want to run our group anymore or how the dynamic would change without Bruce. But our goal was to help Elisa—somehow! We prayed that the Holy Spirit would strengthen us and help us provide for her.
>
> I took heart in the fact that I was studying Acts (through "Drivetime Devotions") and reminded myself and the group that Jesus did not choose the best scholars or smartest people to start his church. Many of the most powerful people in the early church were not the most likely to be successful on paper. So we had faith that somehow God would use our group of self-proclaimed "losers" to help Elisa.
>
> I think it worked!! Our group is stronger than ever. Elisa is an amazing woman, and her strength and faith are a lesson to all of us. She has trusted in God through this time, and the outcome of that trust has been an incredible peace despite this incredibly horrific event. The fact that we even can share moments of joy with her is nothing short of miraculous. Each week we hear a new way that people's lives have been changed because of Bruce and Elisa's witness.
>
> I have never seen a more concrete example of God working in someone's life as I see in Elisa. In fact, the other day she admitted that the way she was handling things and getting through each day was not "humanly possible"; it was possible only through her connection to Jesus, who gives her strength, and our small group. We have also tried to pray for her and with her and provide support in many ways.

We miss Bruce. His absence is still so fresh, but somehow God is providing Elisa's "daily bread" as well as our group's.

We did the four-week "Holy Spirit Foundations" session. Now we have decided that we want to do a grief and loss study together. In your original email to me, you mentioned a book called *Shattered Dreams*. This comes with a companion workbook, so I emailed Elisa and the group yesterday to see if people would like to use that as our next small group series. Thanks for your help and guidance.

Jocelyne

Your small group is designed by God, and you are a critical piece in his eternal equation. Do not give up! Check out this verse: "Let us not give up meeting together, as some are in the habit of doing, but let us encourage one another—and all the more as you see the Day approaching" (Heb. 10:25).

Encourage each other. Find another group leader in your church or ministry so you can learn from and develop each other. This ministry you have isn't designed for you to fly solo.

In Closing

As I write these last few sentences, I pray that something in this book will help you to be more effective in serving our heavenly Father and building his kingdom. You may not do everything like Saddleback does. You may not like our methodology. That's okay! But don't miss the opportunity to use some of the principles in this book to develop your own strategies. I encourage you and your individual members to live out the Great Commission and the Great Commandment.

Please don't let the enemy paralyze you with fear or isolate you. Use this book, connect with your church leadership, use the Small Group Network at www.smallgroupnetwork.com, or email me at steve@stevegladen.com. You matter to God, and leading and building health in your small group is an incredible and eternal privilege.

──────────── ACTION STEPS ────────────

1. Who's really in charge? Are you getting instructions and taking the lead from your heavenly Father, or do you have your own agenda?

_____

_____

_____

2. How do you measure your self-worth? Is it by the things you do, the things you have, or the people you influence? Are your standards of worth the same as God's?

_____

_____

_____

3. Who are you? Are you willing to embrace your role as leader and make the necessary changes to keep improving on your leadership style?

_____

_____

_____

4. What will you do with your life? You have a limited amount of time on this earth; how will you spend your days?

_____

_____

_____

5. How far are you willing to go? Are you 100 percent committed to fulfilling God's purpose for your life? If

so, what is one thing you can do today to continue on your path? If not, what will it take for you to reach a full commitment?

Index

Steve Gladen attended Evangel University in Springfield, Missouri, where he earned a BA in biblical studies with minors in Greek and philosophy. From there he moved to Pasadena, California, and received a master's of divinity from Fuller Theological Seminary, with a concentration in pastoral counseling. While completing his master's, Steve was awarded an internship at a local church in the San Fernando Valley, which started his full-time pastoral career in 1982. Influenced by the small group model taught at Fuller, Steve began to realize the value of small groups in connecting people to the church and in the discipleship process. Throughout his ministry and in churches of varying denominations and sizes, he has successfully implemented the small group strategy in youth ministry, singles ministry, and overall church structures.

Steve joined the staff of Saddleback Church in February of 1998 as pastor of small groups. He oversees the strategic launch and development of the small group community. In 2006 he founded the Small Group Network, a network for leaders of small group ministry (www.smallgroupnetwork. com). Using the Great Commission and great commandment as inspiration, Steve encourages every group member to balance the five biblical purposes in their soul and groups.

Steve has authored *Small Groups with Purpose* and co-authored *250 Big Ideas for Purpose Driven Small Groups*, *Don't Lead Alone*, the *Spiritual Health Assessment and Spiritual Health Planner*, and the Small Group Leader Training Kit. Steve is the general editor for Small Group Life series, which is an eight-volume curriculum set with twelve lessons in each volume. He is also the co-teacher of *Building Biblical Community*, a four-week DVD starter curriculum for small groups. For more information on these resources, go to www. smallgroups.net.

Steve does consulting and seminars throughout the United States and internationally, championing small groups and teaching what it means to have small groups with purpose. Steve and his wife, Lisa, reside in Southern California, have been married since 1989, and have two children, Erika and Ethan. You can stay in touch with Steve at www.stevegladen. com.

RESOURCES from Saddleback and
other leading
small group ministries

At the small group ministries website, you'll find lots of helpful resources.

Over 100 free downloadable resources

The top resources used at Saddleback
   - to build your ministry
   - to train your leaders
   - to build health in your small groups

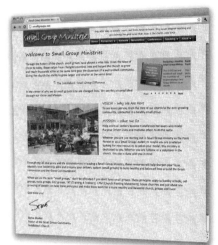

SMALL GROUP *INSIGHTS*™

Where Real Relationships Start

Successful small group experiences despend on authentic relationships. The better the connections, the better the group. And that's just what this tool will do for you.

- Simple
- Personalized
- Engaging
- Quick

Whatever your group's purpose, the Small Group Insights Profile provides you with a fast-track to authenticity and meaningful connection.

www.smallgroupinsights.com

SADDLEBACK CHURCH
Equipping the next generation of small group leaders

Saddleback Church has designed a unique one-year residency internship program (the School of Church Leadership) for small group pastors and leaders. Residents are provided the opportunity to train and learn from Saddleback's small group team while getting hands-on ministry leadership experience.

Unique to the School of Church Leadership is the opportunity to live on our Rancho Capistrano campus. Living in community on "The Ranch" provides a way for resident interns to deepen their learning. Residents will have frequent opportunities to share ideas, empathize with common concerns, and communicate with friends and social networks. Most of all, they will explore their passion—with passion!

Email: Director of Enlistment
LeadershipSchool@Saddleback.com

 Twitter: @SB_SoCL
 Facebook: Saddleback Church School of Church Leadership

HOW TO GROW YOUR CHURCH'S SMALL GROUP MINISTRY

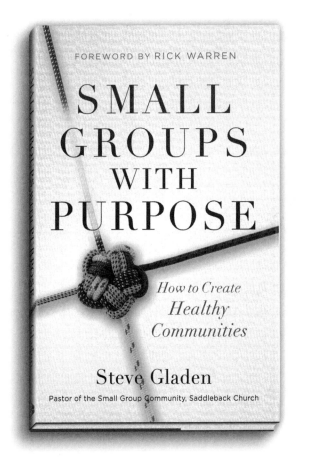

This practical book walks you through the questions you need to answer to develop your own intentional small group strategy. Because it is built on principles and not methods, this step-by-step process can be implemented successfully in any size church.

BakerBooks

Relevant. Intelligent. Engaging.